# A COMPENDIUM OF
# THE DOCTRINES OF GENESIS 1-11

# A COMPENDIUM OF
# THE DOCTRINES OF GENESIS 1-11

**BROTHER CHARLES MADDEN, OFM, CONV..**

iUniverse, Inc.
Bloomington

# A Compendium of the Doctrines of Genesis 1-11

Copyright © 2012 by Brother Charles Madden, OFM, Conv..

All rights reserved. No part of this book may be used or reproduced by any means, graphic, electronic, or mechanical, including photocopying, recording, taping or by any information storage retrieval system without the written permission of the publisher except in the case of brief quotations embodied in critical articles and reviews.

iUniverse books may be ordered through booksellers or by contacting:

iUniverse
1663 Liberty Drive
Bloomington, IN 47403
www.iuniverse.com
1-800-Authors (1-800-288-4677)

Because of the dynamic nature of the Internet, any web addresses or links contained in this book may have changed since publication and may no longer be valid. The views expressed in this work are solely those of the author and do not necessarily reflect the views of the publisher, and the publisher hereby disclaims any responsibility for them.

Any people depicted in stock imagery provided by Thinkstock are models, and such images are being used for illustrative purposes only.
Certain stock imagery © Thinkstock.

ISBN: 978-1-4759-3569-1 (sc)
ISBN: 978-1-4759-3570-7 (ebk)

Printed in the United States of America

iUniverse rev. date: 07/06/2012

# INTRODUCTION

At the start of this series on Creation and the sixteen doctrines in Genesis it is important to note, as Fr. Warkulwiz points out, that there are three degrees of doctrine. First are those doctrines to be believed as divinely revealed (see attached). These doctrines are contained in the Word of God, written or orally transmitted, and defined with a solemn judgment as divinely revealed truth, either by the Pope speaking *ex cathedra*, or by the College of Bishops gathered in council, or infallibly proposed for belief by the ordinary and universal Magisterium of the Bishops in union with the Pope.

Second, to be held definitively, is assent to this kind of doctrine based on faith in the Holy Spirit's assistance to the Magisterium, and on the Catholic doctrine of infallibility of the Magisterium. Third is authoritative non-definitive teaching: a teaching on faith and morals that is presented as true, or at least as sure, even though it has not been defined with a solemn judgment or proposed as definitive by the ordinary and universal Magisterium.

Prior to his election as Pope, Benedict XVI pointed out the need for a Catholic theology of creation. In May 1989 he said: "I must draw attention to the almost total disappearance of the theology of the doctrine of creation. In this connection, it is symptomatic that in the two Summas of modern theology, teaching of creation as contained in the faith is omitted and replaced by vague considerations of existential philosophy . . . . The decline in metaphysics has accompanied the decline in the doctrine of creation." Fr. Warkulwiz points out that this state of affairs is in part caused by the confusion in Catholic circles brought about by the theory of evolution, which seeks to explain the origin of all things by natural causes only. Attempts to construct a coherent theory of "theistic" evolution have foundered, but that aspect will be covered in more detail later.

A sound theology of origins depends on a sound interpretation of Scripture, as the Popes from Leo XIII on have pointed out. He looked upon the Fathers of the Church as the safest guide for interpreting Scripture. In his letter on Scripture "Providentissimus Deus," Pope Leo XIII also said, "It is not forbidden, when just cause exists, to push inquiry and exposition beyond what the Fathers have done." But in doing so, he said, we must always observe "the rule so wisely laid down by St. Augustine—not to depart from the literal and obvious sense, except only where reason makes it untenable or necessity requires; a rule to which it is more necessary to adhere to strictly in these times, when the thirst for novelty and unrestrained freedom of thought make the danger of error most real and proximate." The great majority of the Fathers interpreted Genesis 1-11 in its plain sense. But many Catholic scholars over the last century retreated from that position, thinking that "necessity" required them to do so, as they accepted as "facts" erroneous opinions put forth in the name of science.

The views of the Fathers towards Genesis reigned supreme until the 19th century. For example, it was widely held by theologians and scientists that the great flood in Noah's time produced the sedimentary rock strata existing throughout the earth. In 1830, Charles Lyell rejected the Genesis account and theorized instead that the geological features of the earth could be explained in terms of CURRENT geological processes working over immense periods of time (theory of uniformitarianism), popularized in the expression, "The present is key to the past." Scientists began to think of the age of the earth in terms of millions of years rather than thousands of years.

About 30 years later, Charles Darwin's theory of evolution began to take hold. Because of problems with his ideas of natural variation of properties and natural selection (for example, the lack of intermediate forms between species in the fossil record), Darwinism has fallen into disrepute, at last, and many evolutionists have gone to neo-Darwinism, proposing mutations as the cause of heritable essential changes in organisms. However, facts discovered by modern day biology have demonstrated problems with that idea. After Darwin, the idea of a Creator starting the whole process was dropped by many evolutionists, and evolutionary thought went from simply organic evolution to an all-encompassing materialistic cosmic evolution referred to as molecules-to-man evolution. Some Christians adhere to a theistic form of evolution and reformulate the creation story from Genesis into some form of allegory, completely ignoring the plain sense of Genesis 1-11. Among these the most prominent was Rev. Pierre Teilhard de Chardin, a French Jesuit and paleontologist. His theistic evolutionary views clashed with Catholic teachings on creation, redemption, sanctification, original and actual sin, evil and grace, but were and are today accepted by many, despite repeated condemnations by the Vatican, starting in 1957 right up to 2003, when his writings were cited as being the most popular among adherents of the New Age movement.

Although Darwinism was rejected by many Catholics, the acceptance by some of the theory of uniformitarianism (a great age of the earth, with the fossil record in the rocks being formed by presently-observed natural processes operating over long periods of time) made their position awkward. They rejected the doctrine of six days of creation and the geological principle of catastrophism associated with a great world-wide flood. They cited the Pontifical Biblical Commission's ruling of 1909 allowing the Hebrew word "yom" to be interpreted either as literally one day or a "certain space of time". In recent decades works such as "The Genesis Flood" have gone a long way toward restoring acceptance of the traditional interpretation of Genesis with regard to the age of the earth, the six literal days of creation, and the flood of Noah's time by pointing out the major flaws in the geological theory of uniformitarianism . There is now an abundance of literature written by scientists showing that Genesis does not conflict with the findings of science. This view is resisted by not a few Catholics in scientific and theological circles, lest they be labeled as backward fundamentalists for accepting the Genesis account of six days of creation.

The theory of evolution undermines and confuses the belief of the young in the reliability of Scripture because it differs markedly from the Creation account in Genesis. The words of Pope Leo XIII in Providentissimus Deus are prescient: "For the young, if they lose their reverence for the Holy Scripture on one or more points, are easily led to give up believing in it altogether." Yet in recent years, as will be demonstrated in future classes, non-evolutionary scientists have shown that the actual facts of science are much better explained by the creation and flood accounts in Genesis than by the various theories of evolution. At the present moment, macro-evolution is the politically correct theory for conducting scientific inquiry. Although Pope Pius XII called for a fair hearing on the evolution/creation issue, the discussion has been dominated by one-sided propaganda in favor of evolution. Theistic evolutionists who try to "marry" evolution with the Genesis account of creation simply are not convincing. The Fathers of the Church, who were familiar with the Greek atomists' idea of the universe being formed over eons of time by natural forces, rejected it. Modern day evolutionary theories (there are several theories of evolution extant) are simply a different version of the ideas of the Greek atomists.

# DOCTRINE ONE

## A Personal Supreme Being
## Exists and has revealed Himself

God revealed His existence in Genesis, which was composed by Moses under the inspiration of the Holy Spirit. Moses probably used written documents from both the pre—and post-Flood eras. The Council of Trent affirmed the divine authorship of Genesis, and the Pontifical Biblical Commission in 1906 upheld the Mosaic authorship of Genesis. That God revealed His existence is a category 1 doctrine, de fide credenda. Vatican I decreed that God's existence can be known "with certitude by the light of human reason from created things." It also formally defined the existence of God and condemned as heresy the denial of God's existence.

Genesis says that God conversed with Adam and Eve and made known His will to them. They passed on their knowledge of God, their origin, and the origin of the world to their descendants. Seth and the succeeding pre-Flood patriarchs passed this knowledge on to Noah. Cain and his descendants had this same knowledge, as well. Men believed in only one God, and both polytheism and atheism did not arise until after the Flood.

The question of the human authorship of the books of the Bible must be distinguished from questions of inspiration and inerrancy. These have been clearly defined and repeatedly affirmed by the Church's Magisterium. Though the Church has made no definitive statement concerning authorship of the books of the Bible, the PBC in 1906, as

1

was mentioned earlier, upheld Moses as the author of the Pentateuch, the first five books of the Bible. The Commission said he had direct revelation from God and may have edited or paraphrased existing sources under divine inspiration. He wrote in his own hand, or used scribes, or authorized the final product produced by others under his direction. The PBC allows for glosses and explanations by subsequent inspired writers to be added to the original text. You will see in the last chapter of Deuteronomy, for example, the account of Moses' death.

Fr. Warkulwiz gives a long description of the Documentary Hypothesis controversy with its denial of Moses as the author of the Pentateuch. The theory proposes multiple authors using materials from many different periods, some very old and some not so old, that were rearranged and rewritten by an unknown number of anonymous inspired authors. Even today, there is no real agreement among the Hypothesis' adherents concerning who wrote what. Its presuppositions reflect something of the evolutionary ideology of its day. The all-embracing idea of evolution, whether consciously or unconsciously, is applied to the books of the Bible, whereby the origin of the books begins to imitate the evolution of living species. The DH is a theory involving much speculation but little documentary support. In the 1970s, 17,000 clay tablets were found in the ancient city of Ebla, dating back to 2,500 BC, or about 1,000 years before Moses. One of the claims of the DH proponents is that the names of El and YHWH (YAHWEH) came after Moses' time, but yet are found in these tablets. Modern day discoveries show that writing was indeed very common long before Moses' time, but fail to persuasively support the idea that the Hebrew religious records were not put into writing until after the death of Moses.

The Pentateuch claims Moses as the author (see Ex. 17:14). The New Testament does likewise, as it contains numerous statements by Jesus himself (see John 5:46-47; also, Mark 10:5, Mark 12:26, Luke 24:27, and John 7:19). As Fr. Warkulwiz points out, there are many other flaws in the theory. For instance, modern linguistics supports Moses as the author of Genesis. In the early 1980s, a computer analysis of Genesis done at the Technion Institute in Israel concluded that "It is most probable that the Book of Genesis was written by one person." He also cites the well-respected biblical scholar Msgr. John Steinmuller, who said: "Those passages which are directly attributed to Moses by Sacred Scripture must be believed by DIVINE FAITH to have Moses as their author, and the substance of the other parts of the Pentateuch is THEOLOGICALLY CERTAIN to be of Mosaic origin. Hence, it would be an ERROR IN FAITH to deny the Mosaic origin of those passages of the Pentateuch which are directly attributed to him, and it would be at least TEMERARIOUS to deny the Mosaic origin of those parts which constitute the substance of the Pentateuch."

Concerning the literal-historical truth of Genesis 1-11, there is no evidence whatsoever within those texts that they are anything other than what Moses presented them as, namely, a literal-historical document. This is the unanimous understanding of the Fathers of the Church, which they received from the Apostles, who received it from Christ. The liturgy of the Church confirms that this is genuine Catholic Tradition. The PBC in 1909 rejected arguments denying the literal historical nature of Genesis 1-3, which, by the way, covers thirteen of the sixteen doctrines of Genesis. It rejected the idea that these chapters contain legends, part history or part fiction composed for the edification of souls. It did allow for manifest use of figurative language, such as that which is currently used in modern English; it was never meant to be used to rewrite the text in such a way as to change its basic meaning. It is said that teaching natural science is not the purpose of the Bible. While true, that does not mean biblical assertions about the natural world are subject to reinterpretations contradictory to the literal-historical meaning of the words. It is necessary to interpret Scripture with faith in its accuracy, rather than reinterpret it so as to forge an agreement with contemporary scientific conventions.

# DOCTRINE TWO

## God Created the Whole World from Nothing

This is a very short summary of 60 pages of the text. God's creation of the world from nothing is a divinely revealed doctrine. It was formally confirmed by the 4th Lateran Council in 1215, and again by Vatican Council I in 1870. The 4th Lateran Council also affirmed that God ALONE created the world. Although Genesis does not give an account of the creation of the angels, Sacred Scripture implies and Sacred Tradition holds that they were created "IN THE BEGINNING." The 4th Lateran Council and Vatican Council I formally declared that the angels were created from nothing at the beginning of time. In 1329, Pope John XXII condemned the notion that God created an eternal world. Pope Pius XII clearly stated that natural science is unable to give assured answers concerning the origin of the world.

The first verse of Genesis states: "In the beginning, God created the heavens and the earth." The Hebrew verb translated "created" is "bara," which is used in Scripture exclusively for divine activity. It always has God as its subject. It is never associated with matter out of which God produces something. In Genesis 1:1 and elsewhere in the Hebrew Scriptures, it expresses creation out of nothing (creation ex nihilo). "In the beginning" means that creation marks the start of time and the course of history. The history of the world began at the beginning of Creation Week; and the history of man began at the end of Creation Week, when God created man and gave him dominion over the world.

Since Genesis is an historical document that tells what happened at the very beginning of time, there is no such thing as "pre-history."

The Fathers of Holy Church gave long detailed homilies on the six days of Creation. Foremost are those of St. Basil the Great and St. Ambrose. St Ephrem, St. Augustine and St John Chrysostom also preached and wrote extensively on the Book of Genesis. They regarded creation of the world out of nothing as a basic truth of the Catholic faith. They defended it against the pagan doctrine of dualism and also against Manichaeism. Dualism asserted that there were two eternal and independent realities, spirit and matter. The Manicheans held that there were two sources of creation, the one good and the other evil. One author cites 41 passages from the Fathers affirming that God created all things from nothing. Throughout history, Jews and Christians alike have been certain that the creation of the world out of nothing is directly expressed in the first line of Genesis: "In the beginning, God created the heavens and the earth." The words "In the beginning" have always been taken to mean the absolute beginning, when things other than God began to exist along side Him.

The Church has repeatedly professed in her creeds, conciliar decrees and papal documents that God created (or made) all things. In most of her proclamations ex nihilo is not stated, but it is implied. In 1215, the 4th Lateran Council made the first explicit statement, saying that God created "out of nothing." Lateran 4 was responding to the Cathars, who claimed that a good deity created the world of the spirit, and an evil god was the author of the material world. The First Vatican Council, in opposing the errors of the nineteenth century, again explicitly affirmed that God created the world ex nihilo, emphasizing with an anathema that He created it in its totality.

With regard to the creation of the angels, Genesis is not specific. Some Fathers (e.g., St. Gregory Nazianzen, St. Athanasius, and St. Ambrose) held that the angels were created before the corporeal world. Others, like St. Augustine and St Epiphanius of Salamis, held that they were created at the same time. The 4th Lateran Council later declared that the angels were created from nothing at the beginning of time. It stated that God "from the beginning of time made at once (simul) out of nothing both orders of creatures, that is, the angelic and the earthly . . . ." Vatican Council I reinforced this teaching by quoting the Lateran IV declaration.

The act of creation added nothing to God and subtracted nothing from Him. He continuously holds the world in existence. St. Bonaventure said that God's continuous creative presence in creatures is like a seal leaving its imprint on running water for as long as it is impressed on it. The Church has also condemned the idea that things have "arisen" or "emanated" from the substance of God and the idea that the world was made by a being or beings other than God.

In the purely materialistic form of the theory of evolution, the distinction of creatures is an upward movement of undifferentiated matter/energy towards more organized forms, an ascent to greater perfection. The process is driven by natural causes alone, and the spiritual is just an epiphenomenon (symptom) of highly organized matter. Contrasting with evolutionism is emanationism. In emanationism, the distinction of creatures is a downward movement, from the infinitely perfect to the less perfect. It is a descent from God to spiritual beings to material beings. Emanation is an alleged cosmogonic process proposed as an explanation for the origin of things. It holds that all things proceed from the same divine substance, either immediately or mediately. Although the divine substance loses nothing of its perfection, it does give of its substance. An analogy is a reservoir pouring water into a river. The reservoir shares its substance (water) without losing its perfection of being a continuous reservoir, *ad infinitum*. Also, the process of emanation employs intermediates. Using the above analogy, the river would produce other things, such as streams, by the inherited powers of its waters. Emanationism was widely professed by non-Christian philosophers and theologians in the Middle Ages.

Emanationism conflicts with Catholic doctrine in three ways. First, it holds that God did not produce things ex nihilo but from His own substance. Vatican Council I, in addition to affirming Lateran Council IV teaching that God created from nothing, anathematized those who "say that finite things, both corporeal and spiritual, or at least spiritual, have emanated from the divine substance." Second, emanationism holds that the emanation of things from God's substance is a necessary process because it proceeds from God's nature. God did not produce the world voluntarily but automatically. Thus emanationism denies that God created freely, a doctrine held in Catholic Tradition and formally defined by the First Vatican Council. Third, the theory uses intermediate causes in the emanation of creatures, thus denying immediate creation of creatures by God. It was pointed out earlier that God alone created the world and that no creature is able to participate in God's work of creating ex nihilo. There is a Christian sense in which the word "emanation" is used. It means to come directly from God as a source without implying that He gives of His own substance. St. Thomas Aquinas used the word in a broad sense to include creation: ". . . we must consider not only the emanation of a particular being from a particular agent, but also the emanation of all being from the universal cause which is God; and this emanation we designate by the name of creation."

St. Bonaventure neatly summarizes Catholic Tradition on the creation of the world, pointing out that a vestige of the Creator is found in all creatures: "We must in general understand the following statements about the production of things, for by them truth is found and error refuted. When we say the world is made in time, we exclude the error of those who posit an eternal world. When we say that the world was made out of nothing, we exclude the error of positing an eternity with regard to the material principle. When we say the world was made by a single principle, we exclude the error of the Manicheans who posit a plurality of principles. When we say the world was made by one unaided and supreme, we exclude the error of positing that God has created lesser creatures through the ministration of intelligences."

The Fathers taught that the material world could not exist eternally alongside God because that would make it equal to God in some way. For example, Tatian the Syrian said: "Matter is not without a beginning, like God, nor is it of equal power with God, through being without a beginning." The creation of the world was such a unique and stupendous event that even "miracle" isn't a proper word for it. That word implies a violation or suspension of the laws of nature. In the act of creation, God created the laws of nature. Creation was the event that gave birth to history. For certitude about it, we need the clear testimony of an unimpeachable witness. We have such testimony in the Book of Genesis because it is the word of the Creator Himself.

There are many theories, or cosmologies, of how the universe began. Fr. Warkulwiz goes through a number of them (his field is physics), including a couple that are in accord with Genesis. The most popularized one over recent decades is the big bang theory. According to that theory, the universe was a superdense concentration of matter. The beginning of its separation or explosion was the "big bang," after which the universe evolved to its present state. Theorists can offer no reason for the big bang, which is a serious weakness of the theory. My position is that, in accordance with the notion popular among evolutionists that the present is the key to the past, present-day processes regarding explosions should apply to the big bang. Present day processes regarding explosions always leave us with debris, destruction and chaos; never does something new or higher evolve out of explosions, such as detonation of a blockbuster or a volcanic eruption!

# DOCTRINE THREE

## God Created a Good World

The Council of Florence declared that the Three Persons of the Holy Trinity are one principle of creation. Sacred Scriptures and the Fathers proclaim that God in His wisdom created everything for a good purpose. The Council of Florence and Vatican Council I stated that God created out of His goodness. Vatican I also confirmed the Catholic teaching that God created with perfect freedom. The Provincial Council of Cologne declared that God was free to create this or any other world. Lateran IV and the Council of Florence formally affirmed the scriptural teaching that God's creatures are good in nature. It is de fide teaching that the Three Divine Persons are one, single common principle of creation. It was attested to frequently by the Fathers, and expressed succinctly by the Council of Florence: "the Father and the Son and the Holy Spirit are not three principles of creation but one principle." The Catechism of the Church affirms this in Articles 258, 290-292 and 316.

St. Bonaventure pointed out that the Trinity is the single threefold cause of all things: "since the principle from which the perfection of the universe proceeds is most perfect, it must act from itself, according to itself, and because of itself since in none of its actions does it need anything outside of itself—it must have, with regard to any creature, the force of a three-fold cause, namely efficient, exemplary, and final; it is even necessary that every creature be related to the first cause according to this threefold condition."

The Catechism teaches that God created "according to his wisdom." "O Lord how manifold are thy works! In wisdom thou has made them all; the earth is full of thy creatures", Scripture says. The catechism says the world is not the product of any necessity whatever, nor of blind fate or chance, negating any form of atheistic evolution, and appearing to negate any theistic evolution that tries to use random processes to explain the world's origin. The world didn't just happen to be.

St. Augustine affirms that God created everything for a good purpose, even those things that may be harmful if wrongly used, and even if we cannot always discern the purposes. "Divine Providence thus warns us not to indulge in silly complaints about the state of affairs, but to take pains to inquire what useful purposes are served by things. And when we fail to find the answer, either through deficiency of insight or of staying power, we should believe that the purpose is hidden from us, as it was in many cases where we had great difficulty in discovering it. There is a useful purpose in the obscurity of purpose; it may serve to exercise our humility or to undermine our pride."

God was moved by His goodness to create the world. The Fathers testify to this. His fullness of existence and perfect bliss excluded any other motive. St. Augustine said: "God did not create under stress of any compulsion, or because he lacked something for His own needs; His only motive was goodness; He created because His creation was good." St. Gregory Nazianzen said that it was in God's nature to pour out his goodness: "Since a movement of contemplation to Self could not alone satisfy the Goodness that is God, and since it was the part of the Highest Goodness that good must be poured out and go forth in multiplying the objects of its beneficence, He first conceived the angelic and heavenly powers." St John Damascene and St. Thomas Aquinas made similar comments.

The world was created to the glory of God. The Fathers taught that God created so that his perfections may be manifested and acknowledged. For example, St. Theophilus of Antioch said: "And God has made all things out of those which were not into those which are, so that by his works His greatness may be known and understood." The Catechism (nos. 293-294) teaches: "Scripture and Tradition never cease to teach and celebrate this fundamental truth: 'The world was made for the glory of God.' . . . The glory of God consists in the realization of this manifestation and communication of his goodness, for which the world was created . . . . The ultimate purpose of creation is that God 'who is the creator of all things may at last become 'all in all' thus simultaneously assuring his own glory and our beatitude.'"

The glorification of God that is made by creatures is called external glory. Of this there are two kinds. First, objective glory is the glory given to God by all creatures by virtue of their existence, for in this they mirror the divine perfections. Second, formal glory is the glory given to God by intelligent creatures, which can render it to Him with knowledge and free will. The secondary purpose of the creation of the world is the communication of His goodness, the bestowal of good upon creatures, especially intelligent creatures. God gave man dominion of the works of creation, but this was not to be the ultimate source of his happiness; that was to be the glorification of God.

God created the world free from exterior compulsion and inner necessity. Psalm 139 says, "Whatever the Lord pleases he does, in heaven and on earth, in the seas and all deeps." St. Augustine and other Fathers have pointed this out. For example, St. Irenaeus said that God "made all things freely and spontaneously." The Church's dogma concerning God's freedom in creating clearly concludes that God was not obliged to create the best of all possible worlds. God certainly did not owe it to His creatures to create the best possible world for them. And He didn't owe it to Himself because his perfections and happiness cannot be increased by even the best world. St Bonaventure also pondered the question of whether God created the best of all possible worlds. Etienne Gilson, summing up St. Bonaventure's thought on the subject, said: "The world in which we live is certainly therefore the best possible, but, such as it is, its perfection lacks nothing." He says in part, "If God had made a better world, we could always ask why He had not made one still better . . . God has created the actual world because He has willed and He alone knows the reason of it; we know that what He has given, He has given by pure grace, in an act of goodness which allows of no dissatisfaction; the rest is His secret . . . ."

A total of seven times, then, chapter 1 of Genesis proclaims the goodness of the things God created. Such an emphasis was probably added to highlight the fact that, despite the entrance of evil with the Fall, the world is intrinsically good because it is God's work. The Council of Florence declared that God's creatures are "good indeed, since they were made by the highest good." God did not create evil natures. St. Augustine said: "He does not create evil natures and substances insofar as they are natures and substances." He also said: "There is no such entity in nature as 'evil'; 'evil' is merely a name for the privation of good." Lateran Council IV stated that even "the devil and other demons were created by God good in nature, but they themselves through themselves have become wicked." And the Council of Florence asserted that "nature is not evil, since all nature, insofar as it is nature, is good."

People object to this view because there is so much imperfection and suffering in the world. An adequate reply to this objection requires a careful inquiry into the meanings of the terms "imperfection" and "suffering."

Perfection is measured in terms of what God intended a creature to achieve, not in terms of our perception of perfection. Even a creature that we perceive to have defects in its nature could be perfect in that it achieves the end God intended. Catholic doctrine holds that the goodness of creatures comes from the fact that creation is an outpouring of the goodness of God. The goodness of creatures resides in their relationship to God, that He gave them participation in existence, and not in their own perfection, completeness or perfection.

God is the source of good but not evil in things, although He does allow evil so that He may bring forth good, even greater good, out of it. God created a perfect world in the beginning. Everything achieved the end for which He intended, until man sinned. By sin, man—through his power of free choice that God gave him for the purpose of his freely returning God's love—chose to oppose God's plan of creation. He therefore upset the balance that God had created with detrimental effects on himself, his progeny and the world around him. The original integrity, harmony and order that God created were damaged by sin.

Evil is the absence of good. Every sin removes some of the good in creation by putting holes in its uniform fabric of goodness, so to speak.

Human suffering is an evil because it is a deprivation of a good. It is the deprivation of internal peace and harmony that is necessary for the perfection of the human person. That lack of perfection interferes with God's plan for man. It is not what God originally intended. God allows the wicked to suffer as just punishment and to bring them back to Him. He allows the innocent to suffer because somehow this patches the holes that sin has put in the fabric of goodness. How it does so is a mystery. Romans 11:33 says, "How unsearchable are his judgments and how inscrutable his ways." But we know that the suffering of the just is not in vain and that it will be more than compensated, in eternity. We have the example of Jesus Christ to prove that.

# DOCTRINE FOUR

## God Created Each Thing
## in the World Immediately

Genesis clearly teaches that God created each thing during Creation Week entirely and instantly, without the intervention of another agent. The Fathers and Doctors of the Church all believed that. There is no good reason for a Catholic to deny it. Natural science cannot speak authoritatively on this issue because it is beyond the competence of its methods.

Each thing that God created during Creation Week, He created instantly in its entirety, with the suddenness of Christ's miracles. In Genesis God commands, and one object after another leaps into existence. Thus He created the earth, its creatures, the stars, the galaxies and other celestial objects in the form we see them today. That does not mean that He created a static world. It is obvious that He created a dynamic world, an ever-changing world. But He created a whole, finished world and set it in operation. This is the teaching of Genesis. It can be interpreted no other way without violating the text.

This is what the Fathers of the Church unanimously believed. They often repeated that God created immediately and instantly. For example, St. Ephrem the Syrian compared the speed of God's acts of creation on the first day to the length of that day: "Although both the light and the clouds were created in the twinkling of an eye, still both the day and night of the first day continued for twelve hours each." He introduces the notion of apparent age—the young look old: "Just as the trees, the vegetation, the animals, the birds and even mankind were old, so also were they young. They were old according to the appearance of their limbs and their substances, yet they were young because of the hour and moment of their creation. Likewise, the moon was both old and young. It was young, for it was but a moment old, but was also old, for it was as full as it is on the fifteenth day."

And concerning the creation of plant life on the third day, he said: "Although the grasses were only a moment old at their creation, they appeared as if they were months old. Likewise, the trees, although only a day old when they sprouted forth, were nevertheless like trees years old as they were fully grown and fruits were already budding on their branches. The grass that would be required as food for the animals two days later was thus made ready."

The Fathers of the Church rejected the idea of a universe being formed by natural forces over eons from primeval matter. St. Ambrose said that when Moses says so abruptly "in the beginning God created" he meant to emphasize the incredible speed of the work. Alluding to the Greek atomists he said: "He (Moses) did not look forward to a late and leisurely creation of the world out of a concourse of atoms." Furthermore, he says, "And fittingly (Moses) added: 'He created.', lest it be thought there was a delay in creation. Furthermore, men would see how incomparable the Creator was Who completed such a great work in the briefest moment of His creative act, so much so that the effect of His will anticipated the perception of time." St. Athanasius also taught that all things in each of the six days were created instantly and simultaneously.

Knowledge concerning the events of Creation Week is beyond the competence of the methods of natural science. This is because the very laws of nature were then being created. St. Basil expresses this in his commentary on the third day of Creation. He even proposed that matter and the laws that govern it are separate creations: "Someone may, perhaps, ask this: Why does the Scripture reduce to the command of the Creator that tendency to flow downward which belongs naturally to water? . . . If water had this tendency by nature, the command ordering the waters to be gathered into one place would be superfluous . . . . To this inquiry we say this, that you recognized very well the movements of the water after the command of the Lord, both that it is unsteady and unstable and that it is borne naturally down slopes and hollows; but how it had any power previous to that, before motion was engendered in it from this command, you yourself neither know nor have you heard it from one who knew. Reflect that the voice of God makes nature, and the command given at that time to creation provided the future course of action for creatures."

Science provides us with some indications. The existence throughout the world of an enormous number of polonium halos in the bedrocks of the earth strongly suggests that these rocks were created fully formed within three minutes. Polonium-218 is a short-lived isotope with a half-life of only three minutes. Primordial polonium-218 atoms have left their fingerprints in the foundation rocks of the earth in the form of spherical shells of discoloration caused by the energetic decay products. When the rocks are sliced thin and viewed under a microscope, the discolorations appear in the form of halos. Since these halos could not have formed in a liquid, they must have been imbedded in the solid rock. And since the lifetime of the polonium atoms is so short, they must have been there when the rocks were made. This implies a nearly instantaneously crystallization of the rocks. Dr. Robert V. Gentry has been studying these rocks for years and sees the polonium halos as strong evidence in favor of instantaneous creation. It should be noted that the issue is not fully settled. And even if it were, the polonium halos would at best provide strong evidence in favor of instantaneous creation but would not "prove" that the rocks were instantly created. One could conceive of other possible, albeit improbable, scenarios to explain their production.

A common objection to this teaching is that we "know" the big bang occurred 10 or 20 billion years ago and the universe evolved as is seen today. This is known as cosmic evolution. The objection is based on this reigning cosmogony of our time. Other cosmogonies have been proposed in the past but only the one in Genesis has endured, and has done so because it is the truth. Despite the immense popularity of the big bang theory, its foundation and structure are weak. And we don't need biblical creationists to point that out. Noncreationist

16

scientists do a good job of that on their own. The big bang theory is simply a theoretical construct based on equations applied far beyond the range of experience; and it is lacking in unimpeachable empirical evidence, despite the claim of its adherents. This does not even take into consideration the fact that the origin of the universe is an historical event, the truth of which can be made known only by the testimony of an eyewitness. Some claim that the beauty of macroevolution is that it unifies our knowledge of nature. They claim that all scientific facts can be related by assuming the beginning was the "big bang," which sent matter flying through space, matter that the forces of nature evolved into the wonder-filled universe we live in today. All this is false and is wishful thinking by those desirous of reducing everything to two great principles: the big bang and macroevolution. It is simply an updated version of Greek atomism and is just as incredible.

The big bang theory does not fit neatly into the cosmic scenario if one takes facts more seriously than ideas. However, the favorable propaganda has been relentless, and its accumulation of adherents despite its inadequacy is the only real success it can claim. As to being a scientific fact, one of its most outstanding proponents, Steven Weinberg, admits: "I cannot deny a feeling of unreality in writing about the first three minutes (after the big bang) as if we really know what we are talking about." And we will see later the notions of biological macroevolution and geological eons fit the facts even less.

Another objection to the teaching of the immediate creation of everything by God is based on the idea that living organisms are the product of millions of years of evolution. Elements spontaneously came together in the primeval atmosphere to form amino acids, the building blocks of living organisms. This process has been demonstrated in the laboratory. Amino acids then spontaneously combined to form proteins, which spontaneously combined to form a living cell, which evolved into more complex living organisms. This emergence of life from nonliving matter does not violate the second law of thermodynamics because life is a statistical fluctuation from the norm, and it is the norm that is governed by that law. The emergence of life is a highly improbable fluctuation, but it had plenty of time to occur.

This objection is based on two assumptions. The first is that the laboratory production of amino acids shows what could have happened on earth. The second is that a living cell is the possible outcome of a statistical fluctuation. An examination of these two assumptions reveals that the creation of life requires the immediate activity of an intelligent power.

Amino acids "spontaneously" produced from nonliving matter in the laboratory are actually produced under contrived conditions that could never be duplicated in a lifeless natural situation because they require the intervention of an intelligent agent. In the laboratory, the experimenter whisks away the amino acid molecules before they can decompose. In a natural environment the same forces that produced the molecules would destroy them long before they had the opportunity of entering into extremely complex combinations with a variety of others to form proteins.

The second law of thermodynamics was originally applied to heat engines. It states that thermal energy cannot be totally converted into mechanical energy or other useful forms. Since various forms of energy are continuously being converted into thermal (disordered) energy, and thermal energy cannot be completely transformed back into ordered (useful) energy, the amount of transformable energy in the universe is continually diminishing. The second law of thermodynamics is rooted in statistics concerning the locations and the motions of the molecules of a material substance, and it states only the most probable situation.

The disordered molecular states open to a substance are essentially indistinguishable from each other and are extremely more numerous than those that can be considered ordered. Therefore disorder is favored. But it is possible for a statistical fluctuation to occur that takes a substance into an ordered molecular state, although the probability for doing so is extremely small. And such states are highly unstable. Yet evolutionists grab at this straw and claim that living organisms could come about by statistical fluctuations in the molecular states of matter. However, they are blowing smoke. Living organisms would then be states that are available by fluctuations. That is, they would be probable outcomes. It is the burden of the evolutionists to prove that they are, since the number of ordered molecular states that are probable outcomes is much less than all the conceivable ordered states. For example, consider trying to assemble an operating watch by throwing all the parts in the air and allowing them to fall on a table. There are an infinite number of ways that the parts can fall on the table, some of them highly ordered. But is one of those ways a wound-up operating watch? Those who would answer yes to that question have the burden of demonstrating it. They would have to establish that the force of gravity acting downward, air resistance, and collisions of parts are adequate to produce all of the forces, torques, twists and turns necessary to produce an operative watch. They would be hard put to present a convincing case. After failing, they would be forced to admit the necessity of an energy conversion mechanism (something that can produce the necessary forces and torques, twists and turns) and a control system that directs the energy conversion (something that directs the forces, torques, twists and turns). The former are the hands of the watchmaker, and the latter are his soul and brain. And this example does not even take into account that the parts themselves have to be properly constructed to work together as a watch. Since a living cell is infinitely more complex than a watch, it would be impossible for anyone to demonstrate that it is a possible outcome of statistical fluctuations.

The second law of thermodynamics is also known as the law of increasing entropy. Entropy is a measure of the amount of thermal energy in a system that is not available to do work. In other words, it is a measure of the amount of disordered energy in a system that cannot be ordered. Entropy, then, is a measure of disorder. The more disordered a system the higher its entropy. A perfectly ordered system has zero entropy. The second law of thermodynamics is expressed in terms of entropy as follows: if an isolated physical system undergoes a process that takes it from one thermodynamic state to another, the entropy of the final state cannot be less than that of the initial state. Most often it is higher. In everyday terms this means that things in the world are continually becoming more disordered. The second law of thermodynamics is to order as the law of gravity is to mass. As the law of gravity causes a ball to roll from states of higher elevation to states of lower elevation, so the second law of thermodynamics causes a physical system to "roll" from states of higher order to states of lower order. The $75,000 car runs less well with age. The million dollar house will deteriorate over time. We can counter this entropy in the car and the house through intelligent intervention but we can only delay it for a time. Only God alone can set aside the second law of thermodynamics and only God alone can create the order manifested in living organisms.

# DOCTRINE FIVE

## God created each living creature according to its kind

Genesis repeatedly states that each living creature was created "according to its kind." The Fathers of Holy Church unanimously believed that the progenitor of each living creature was specially created, that is, was created in its fitting and enduring nature during Creation Week. The scientific facts strongly support this, despite the claims of scientists that life evolved over immense spans of time from simple to more complex forms. The fact that many Catholics today feel free to deny special creation and give more credence to the shaky paradigm of biological evolution than to divine revelation as interpreted by the Church for 2,000 years, indicates a definite devolution of the faith in the modern Church. It is possible that the Church may one day define the special creation of species as revealed truth because it is deeply rooted in Sacred Tradition and sound scriptural exegesis. The same cannot be said for the evolution of species because that has no support whatsoever in Scripture or Tradition.

Charles Darwin concluded his *Origin of Species* with the statement: "There is grandeur in this view of life, with its several powers, having been originally breathed by the Creator into a few forms or into one; and that, whilst this planet has gone cycling on according to the fixed law of gravity, from so simple a beginning endless forms most beautiful and most wonderful have been, and are being evolved." Darwin held that all the living species on earth evolved from one or a few primeval living forms and that contemporary species are slowly transforming into new species. This directly contradicts the Genesis account, which states that all living creatures were created in the beginning "according to their kind." Darwin's "Creator" is not the God of Genesis, nor is Darwin's "grandeur" the glory of God, but is, indeed, the pride of man.

The Fathers of the Church accepted, without question, the fact that each living creature was specially created. St. Ambrose makes the point that many different living creatures were created simultaneously: "At this command the waters immediately poured forth their offspring. The rivers were in labor. The lakes produced their quota of life. The sea itself began to bear all manner of reptiles . . . . We are unable to record the multiplicity of the names of all those species which by Divine command were brought to life in a moment of time. At the same instant substantial form and the principle of life were brought into existence . . . . The whale, as well as the frog, came into existence at the same time by the same creative power."

St. John Chrysostom speaks of the wonder of the fifth day: "Just as He said of the earth only: 'Let it bring forth,' and there appeared a great variety of flowers, herbs and seeds, and all occurred by His word alone, so here also He said: 'Let the waters bring forth swarms of living creatures, and let birds fly above the earth across the firmament of the heavens'—and instantly there were so many kinds of crawling things, such a variety of birds, that one cannot number them in words."

St. Gregory of Nyssa lays to rest the pseudo-paradox: What came first, the chicken or the egg? "In the beginning, we see, it was not an ear rising from a grain but a grain coming from an ear, and after that, the ear grows round the grain."

St. Basil the Great, in discussing the work of the third day, gives the meaning of "according to its kind": "There is nothing truer than this, that either each plant has seed or there exists in it some generative power. And this accounts for the expression 'of its own kind.' For the shoot of the reed is not productive of an olive tree, but from the reed comes another reed, and from seeds spring plants related to the seeds sown. Thus what was put forth by earth in its first generation has been preserved until the present time, since the kinds persisted through constant reproduction."

The nature of an animal or plant is not always easy to define. But we have a strong instinctive sense about their nature that we can't transcribe into words. For example, any child is able to distinguish a dog from a cat, even though there are many varieties of each. The child is able to accurately distinguish "dogness" from "catness" even though he is unable to express the distinction in words. All he could do to distinguish them would be to give accidental features, for example: dogs have wet noses; cats have long whiskers.

The great naturalist Carolus Linneaus (1707-1778) believed in the special creation and permanence of the created kinds, and he tried to distinguish these kinds as best as possible in a system of classification. In his system, the basic unit is the species. The next highest order of ranking is the genus, in which species are grouped according to structural features. Linnaeus assigned a genus and a species to an organism. His system of classification goes by the name binomial nomenclature. Modern naturalists use Linnaeus' system in an expanded form with groupings higher than genus. This system is artificial. It is useful for organizing and identifying living organisms, but it does not give much insight into the natures of the organisms it classifies. Linnaeus himself recognized this.

A natural species is a complete collection of individual organisms that share the same specific essence. This definition recognizes the existence of natural divisions within the plant and animal kingdoms. Since man, being a rational animal, is obviously a natural species, it seems fitting that the other animals and the plants also belong to their own natural species. The created kinds are the natures of the natural species. The natural species are natural groups, and the kinds are the specific natures of those groups. A systematic species is an artificial grouping; it is a collection of individual organisms grouped together according to some convenient criteria. Systematic species are fleeting. They can change according to the circumstances of the question under consideration. Evolutionists work only with systematic species because they do not believe in the immutability of species. The naturalist A. C.

Cotter defines natural species in terms of their purpose in the balance of nature. Some examples; a cow produces milk, sheep furnish wool, bees make honey. Francisco Suarez (1548-1617) said that purpose constitutes and completes the essence of a natural being. He pointed out that some of those features are directed toward the preservation of the individual or the species. But this is again linked to its purpose because the organism is preserved to achieve it. The Catechism #340 confirms this: "God wills the interdependence of creatures. The sun and the moon, the cedar and the little flower, the eagle and the sparrow: the spectacle of their countless diversities and inequalities tells us that no creature is self-sufficient. Creatures exist only in dependence on each other, to complete each other, in the service of each other." This mutual dependence of creatures on one another strongly suggests that all creatures were created together in a short period of time.

Here are some criteria for identifying natural species:

Infertility/Intrasterility—This criterion, in one form or another, is the one most widely used by naturalists. It states that if individual plants or animals have the power to breed offspring identical in nature, and if those offspring and their offspring and so on have the same power, those individuals belong to the same species. This criterion further states that if this power is not present, the individuals belong to different species. This criterion implies sexual reproduction and its biological possibility, but not necessarily its actuality

Likeness of visible characteristics—Differentiating plants and animals by their visible characteristics is the most obvious procedure to follow, and naturalists have developed it in detail. In this way we immediately differentiate between dogs, cats, horses, cows, and so on. Botanists identify plants by their flowers, seeds, fruits, leaves and other characteristics. However, as the saying goes, looks may be deceiving. Things that look alike may be very different, and things that look different may be alike in their nature. Totally unrelated organisms sometimes have similar visible characteristics and related ones dissimilar characteristics.

Life cycle—Individuals of different species follow a different rhythm of life. Members of the same species generally have the same gestation period, the same maturation stages and chronology, and the same natural lifetime, all within limits and with some exceptions, of course.

Instinct—Members of the same animal species display the same specific instinctive behavior. Members of the same species court, mate, rear their young, and procure food in the same way. They follow the same migratory patterns and chronology. Individuals in a community may have different chores but they work together for the same end. For example, the queen, the drones and the workers in a colony of bees each contribute in their own way to produce a hive and honey.

Chromosomes—Another way to differentiate natural species is by the number, size and shape of chromosomes their cells contain. Every species has a definite number of chromosomes, and the number is generally even. The drawback of this method is that there are different species that have the same number of chromosomes. But their size and shape may be different, and ambiguities can often be resolved by macroscopic properties of the species. Also, DNA analysis has become a powerful identification tool.

Let us consider the discontinuity of various species. It is an observed fact. In the world of living organisms and in the fossil world, there are only distinct organisms separated by gaps. Evolutionists are forced by the facts to admit that there are no transitional or intermediate forms in the living world today or in the fossil record. Zoologist Theodosius Dobzhansky states: "If we assemble as many individuals living at a given time as we can, we notice at once that the observed variation does not form any kind of continuous distribution. Instead, a multitude of separate, discrete distributions are found. The living world is not a single array of individuals in which any two variants are connected by unbroken series of intergrades, but show more-or-less distinctly separate arrays, between which intermediates are either absent or at least rare.

Paleontologist George Gaylord Simpson admits noncontinuity in the fossil record: "In spite of these examples, it remains true, as every paleontologist knows, that most new species, genera, and families, and nearly all new categories above the level of families, appear in the record suddenly and are not led up to by known, gradual, and completely continuous transitional sequences." This presents a problem for evolutionists because their theory predicts a continuum of organic forms, but that just doesn't exist. Distinct forms with gaps are exactly what one would expect to observe according to the Genesis account.

Genesis implies the stability of kinds. In Genesis 1 it is said that the plants and animals were created according to their kind. The Fathers of Holy Church believed in the permanence of kinds. For example, St Basil said about "according to their kinds" the following: "Consider the word of God moving through all creation having begun at that time, active up to the present, and efficacious until the end, even to the consummation of the world . . . . .It (nature) begets a horse as a successor of a horse, a lion of a lion and an eagle of an eagle. It continues to preserve each of the animals by uninterrupted successions until the consummation of the universe." The visible characteristics of plants and animals have remained essentially unchanged over the centuries. Aristotle described a number of animals over 2,000 years ago, and his descriptions agree with present-day observations.

One of the objections to the doctrine that God created each living creature according to its kind is that many paleontologists assert not all species of plants and animals originated at one and the same time; but they are not able to prove this, and the evidence indicates otherwise. The objection is based on interpretation of the fossil record. It is rooted in two theories: one, by Georges Culver that fossil bearing strata were laid down by a series of great floods long before man's creation and separated by immense periods of time, the last great flood being in Noah's time. After each flood the surviving animals repopulated the earth again. The second theory, by Charles Lyell, rejected any theory of world wide catastrophes laying down the fossil strata but rather they were laid down by the geological processes of erosion and sedimentation working slowly over immense periods of time (uniformitarianism).

Three facts contradicting these theories are: There are no surface irregularities in the interfaces where the strata meet. Therefore each succeeding stratum in a formation must have been laid shortly after the preceding one because no erosion took place. Also, polystrate fossils are single fossils that pass through more than one stratum. Fossilized upright trees have been found that pass through several strata, the tops and bottoms of the trees sometimes differing in age by millions of years in age according to uniformitarian reckoning. Finally, traditional geology assumes that all strata were laid one on top of the other like a pile of carpets. However, experiments in sedimentology by the French scientist Guy Berthault give a different picture of their formation. They show that when there is a water current present, which is generally the case, strata do not form successively but laterally and vertically at the same time.

Noah's flood in Genesis explains the geological record much better than uniformitarian geology. It explains things difficult for established academic geology to explain such as wave strata, why most rock is sedimentary, and why marine fossils are found on mountains. The fossil record generally, but with many exceptions, contains invertebrates in the lower strata, fish above them, then amphibians, reptiles and mammals. But instead of being evidence for evolution, it is what one would expect if a universal worldwide flood produced the fossil record by pouring successive waves of sediment into the sea. Invertebrates that live on the ocean floor would be buried first, then fish, and so on. The creatures would tend to be buried in the order of the elevation of their habitat and their degree of mobility. The fossil record also shows that life forms have remained essentially unchanged during their history. They have no ancestral forms, and forms that are preserved in the fossil record are either extinct or identical to forms currently living.

Now we consider the geologic column. The geologic column was originally conceived as a division of the layers of rock on the surface of the earth into "systems" of strata, without any age attached. Evolutionists converted the systems from representations of rock formations into historical periods or eras. They dated these systems according to the fossils they contained, based on how long they believed it took for the fossilized creatures to evolve. Fossils found in the rocks are then dated according to the rocks in which they are found, and the geological column is said to demonstrate the evolution of species over millions of years. Such reasoning is circular. Furthermore, the idea that a geologic column of sedimentary rock uniformly covers the face of the earth is an artificial construct. Textbooks present the geologic column with the strata neatly stacked on one another, progressing from the oldest rocks on the bottom to the youngest rocks on the top. This is not an accurate representation of the face of the earth. Geologist S. A. Austin writes: "The notion that the earth's crust has an 'onion skin' structure with successive layers containing all strata systems distributed on a global scale is not according to the facts . . . . The entire geologic column, composed of complete strata systems, exists only in diagrams drawn by geologists."

A striking contradiction to the standard chronology of the geologic column is the fact that there are many areas of rock strata that contain fossils in inverse evolutionary sequence, that is, with the allegedly younger rocks on the bottom and the older rocks on the top. Fr. Warkulwiz gives several examples of this in the American West and the Alps. Another problem with rock dating in the geologic column is that the sedimentary rocks do not contain meteorites, and only a few meteorites have been found below the highest levels of the geologic column, far below what ought to be found if meteorites bombarded the earth over millions of years at the current rate of meteor bombardment.

Fr. Warkulwiz ends this segment with a long discussion on the controversy around Pope John Paul II's statement in 1996 that evolution is more than a hypothesis. There is controversy over the precise wording attributed to the Pope.

# DOCTRINE SIX

## God created the world in six natural days.

Scholars generally agree that the Hebrew word yom used in Genesis 1 was intended by the sacred author to mean a literal natural day and not an indefinite period of time. The great majority of the Church Fathers believed that God created the world in six natural days. None of them professed the belief that God took eons of time to create the world. The Pontifical Biblical Commission in 1909 allowed interpreters of Scripture to argue that yom means "the natural day" or "a certain space of time." But it is out of bounds to assert that "a certain space of time" means undefined millions of years, because this cannot be established as a "necessary" interpretation. Considering that 1) yom is never used in Sacred Scripture for a period of time of definite length other than a natural day, and 2) the hermeneutical principle of Pope Leo XIII that Scripture must be understood in its "literal and obvious sense" unless reason or necessity forces us to do otherwise, and 3) the near-unanimous belief of the Fathers and Doctors of the Church, and 4) that the creation day is the prototype of the natural day, which sets the rhythm for our lives and life on earth in general, and 5) the fact that the natural sciences are unable to confirm or refute it, there is no justification for a Catholic to deny that God created the world in six natural days.

The Catechism #337 says: "Scripture presents the work of the Creator symbolically as a succession of days of divine 'work' concluded by the 'rest' of the seventh day." But that is not to say that the six days and the works of the six days were in themselves not real. For instance, Ezekiel 4, 5, and 12 tells of his performing real actions that had symbolic meaning for the life of Israel. Likewise the work of God in six natural days has symbolic meaning for our lives.

The Fathers of Holy Church took it for granted that each of the six days was a natural day. St. Ephrem the Syrian says: "Although both the light and the clouds were created in the twinkling of an eye, still both the day and the night of the First Day continued for twelve hours each. Although the grasses were only a moment old at their creation, they appeared as if they were months old. Likewise, the trees, although only a day old when they sprouted forth, were nevertheless like old trees, as they were fully grown and fruits were already budding on their branches. The grass that would be required as food for the animals two days later was thus made ready. And the new corn that would be food for Adam and his descendants, who would be thrown out of paradise four days later, was thus prepared."

St Basil considered the first day as setting the standard for the natural day. "'There was evening and morning'. This means the space of a day and a night . . . . 'And there was evening and morning, one day.' Why did he say 'one' and not 'first'? . . . He said 'one' because he was defining the measure of day and night and combining the time of a night and a day, since the twenty-four hours fill up the interval of one day, if, of course, night is understood with day."

St. Ambrose said: "In notable fashion has Scripture spoken of a 'day,' not the 'first day.' Because a second, then a third, day, and finally the remaining days were to follow, a 'first day' could have been mentioned, following in this way the natural order. But Scripture established a law that twenty-four hours, including both day and night, should be given the name of day only, as if one were to say the length of one day is twenty-four hours in extent." Also, St. John Chrysostom, St. Gregory of Nyssa, St. Jerome, and St Gregory the Great, all believed that God created the world successively in six natural days.

In Genesis 1, the Hebrew word 'yom' is used in two of the same ways that we use the English word 'day'; that is, the bright part of the day or a full natural day. The word 'yom' is used 1,904 times in the Hebrew Old Testament, 57 times in Genesis 1-11. It is always used in the same way we use day as just mentioned. Expressions such as Psalm 90 "For a thousand days in thy sight are but yesterday . . ." refer to God's transcending time and not an interpretation of the word 'yom' in Genesis. The days of Creation Week are the archetype of the human work week, and for that reason alone it makes sense that its duration was the same. If Moses wished to convey the idea of periods of time measured in millennia, as theistic evolutionists say, he could have done so clearly using other words, for example, 'olam', which means a long indefinite time.

The Pontifical Biblical Commission in its 1909 responses concerning the interpretation of Genesis 1-3 allowed free discussion by interpreters on the question of whether the word "yom", when used to distinguish the six days in Genesis 1, means strictly "the natural day" or less strictly "a certain space of time." But this freedom must be exercised in accordance with the hermeneutical principle of Pope Leo XIII that Scripture must be understood in its "literal and obvious sense" unless reason or necessity forces us to do otherwise. Therefore, one cannot argue arbitrarily that yom means "a certain space of time" other than a natural day but must establish that it is necessary to interpret it that way. Considering then 1) that yom is never used in Sacred Scripture for a period of time of definite length other than a natural day, 2) the hermeneutical principle of Leo XIII, 3) the nearly universal understanding of the Fathers and their successors, 4) that the creation day is the prototype of the natural day, which sets the rhythm of our lives and life on earth in general, and 5) the fact that the natural sciences are unable to confirm or refute it, it is not reasonable to take the word yom in Genesis 1 to mean other than a literal natural day.

Genesis 1 lists the breakdown of the six days of creation as follows: Day 1—Creation of the heavens, the earth, light, making day and night; Day 2—Separation of waters into two parts, putting an expanse between them; Day 3—Make dry land, gather water into seas, create plant life; Day 4—Create heavenly bodies; Day 5—Create living water creatures, and birds; Day 6—Create living land creatures, and create man. There is symmetry here between the first three days and the last three: Day 1, creation of light, and Day 4, creation of luminous bodies; Day 2, creation of the sea and skies, and Day 5, creation of the occupants of the sea and sky; Day 3, creation of dry land, and Day 6, creation of dry land's inhabitants.

God created light on Day 1, separating it from darkness and calling it "day" and darkness "night", creating them before the sun and the moon. Some can't understand how this can be and dismiss the creation account as myth or allegory. But Genesis says that God created the sun and the moon to "rule" day and night, not to determine them. This means that periods of day and night by their nature precede the sun and the moon. The sun and the moon were created to regulate periods of time that had already been determined. As St. John Chrysostom put it, "He created the sun on the fourth day lest you think that it is the cause of the day." Another question concerns the source of the light created on Day 1, namely, where did it come from if the sun and stars were not yet made? A possible source for the light could have been chemical and nuclear reactions in the raw matter of earth itself. But according to modern physics a source really isn't needed. Light is not tethered to a source. Once a photon of light leaves its source it is free and has an existence of its own. So modern physics has no problem with the idea that God created light without a source, and it has no problem with the fact that He set up a standard of time independent of the sun and the moon.

St. Thomas Aquinas distinguishes three works in his "Treatise on the Work of the Six Days". The work of creation of the heavens and the earth was done on the first day; works of distinction or separation on Days 1, 2, and 3; works of adornment on Days 3-6. Day 1: "In the beginning God created the heavens and the earth." As to works of distinction, on Day 1, "God separated the light from the darkness." On Day 2, He "separated the waters which were under the firmament from the waters which were above the firmament." On Day 3, He separated the land from the waters. We have already discussed the separation of the light from the darkness. As to the firmament he gives two interpretations, the first is the starry firmament, the second not being that in which the stars are set, "but the part of the atmosphere where the clouds are collected and which has received the name 'firmament' from the firmness and density of the air." He holds that there are waters above the firmament. "If, however, we understand by the firmament that part of the air in which the clouds are collected, then the waters above the firmament must rather be the vapors resolved from the waters which are raised above a part of the atmosphere, from which the rain falls." He and St Augustine believed that the waters above the firmament are held there by natural processes and not miraculously. [Fr. Warkulwiz will elaborate upon all the vital functions water plays in our life. He points out, among many things, that God used water to reshape the face of the earth during the Great Flood. The properties of water can no way be construed as accidental. They are part of God's master plan of creation.]

On Day 3 through Day 6, God adorned his work of creation. On Day 3, He created plant life, which would serve as food for other living creatures. The biochemical unity of men, animals and plants is because they all came from the Creator and not because they came from a common ancestor. Each species of plant was created for a purpose, that purpose is not always self-evident. It is noteworthy that Saints Basil, Ambrose and John Chrysostom all point out that they were created before the sun and therefore do not depend on the sun for their origin. On Day 4, God created the heavenly bodies that would regulate the lives of plants and other living creatures.

The cosmos is delicately balanced to serve life on earth. For example, the sun's orbit is inclined to the earth at just the right angle to produce the seasons, and the sun is just the right distance away to keep the earth within a temperature range favorable to life. Small deviations would be disastrous! Astronomers constantly find new wonders reflecting God's great power and majesty. Genesis gives us just the barest outline of His mighty works.

On Day 5, God created living creatures for the sea and air, perhaps just a small number of each, and then telling them to be fruitful and multiply. On Day 6, He created land creatures, culminating in the creation of man, who was created in His own image and likeness and to have dominion over all other creatures. All creatures were created for the use and spiritual benefit of man, as St. John Chrysostom says: "It wasn't simply for our use that He produced all these things; it was also for our benefit in the sense that we might see the overflowing abundance of His creatures and be overwhelmed at the Creator's power, and be in a position to know that all these things were produced by a certain wisdom and ineffable love out of regard for the human being that was designed to come into being."

No new matter or new kinds of living organisms were created after Creation Week. "Thus the heavens and the earth were finished, and all the host of them. And on the seventh day God finished the work he had done . . . ." Even Jesus Christ, in His miracles, did not create ex nihilo. He transformed that which already existed. The only ongoing creation is the creation of human souls. But even that is connected in with the original order of creation. St. Thomas Aquinas says: "Nothing entirely new was afterward made by God, but all things subsequently made had in a sense been made before in the work of the six days. Some things, indeed, had a previous experience materially, as the rib from the side of Adam out of which God formed Eve . . . ."

God rested on the seventh day in that He ceased creating. But His work continues on in His holding the created world in existence and in His governing it through the natural laws that He created. He also governs it directly by revealing His will to men, and by intervening in the course of nature through miracles, both visible and invisible. The seventh day is related to the "Day of the Lord," which is often mentioned in Sacred Scripture. The Day of the Lord is that day when the Lord will come, again, to judge the world and save the faithful. The seventh day is not given an ending like the other days in Genesis. The Fathers of the Church see it as being the archetype of eternal life. For example, St. Augustine says: "Heaven, too, will be the fulfillment of that Sabbath rest . . . ." And St. Ephrem says: "It (the Sabbath) was given to them in order to depict by a temporal rest, which He gave to a temporal people, the mystery of the true rest, which will be given to the eternal people in the eternal world."

Sacred Scripture does not present time as a continuum with the present separating past from future in a uniform advance. That conception of time comes from the Enlightenment thinkers and their mechanical view of nature. Instead, Scripture marks off the passage of time in terms of events of great significance: Creation, The Fall, The Great

Flood . . . The Passover, and so on. And it perceives time as a hierarchy of rhythms: heartbeat, day, week, month, and year. All but the week are based on natural rhythms. The week is a specially created divine rhythm. The week is like a repeating melody, a series of seven musical notes with the accent put on the Sabbath. Everywhere, at all times, people have observed a seven-day week. This presents a problem for those who seek only natural causes for things because there is no natural explanation for it. The day is determined by the rising and the setting of the sun, the month by the phases of the moon, and the year by the elevation of the sun. But there is no natural process that defines the seven-day week. Yet it has existed for thousands of years. The only reasonable explanation is that God ordained the seven-day week, as we are told in Genesis.

Some Catholics erroneously state that St Augustine and St Gregory believed in evolution and that the six days of creation were symbolic, however St Thomas Aquinas states: "Augustine's view is that at first in creation certain things were given existence in their own nature, according to their distinct species, for example, the elements, the heavenly bodies and spiritual substances (angels); but that certain others—such as plants, animals and men—existed only in their germinal principles. Afterward, all of these latter were produced in their distinct types by that operative governance which God, ever since the six days, has continued to exercise upon His original creation." St. Gregory also held that God created everything simultaneously, but indistinctly. He was not a transformist, nor did he hold that the six days were somehow symbolic. He specifically stated he did not contradict anything St. Basil wrote concerning the creation of the world. St. Basil, by the way, strongly upheld the fixity of living species and the literalness of the six days of creation.

Some Catholics say that Genesis 2:4 contradicts the account in Genesis 1, thus implying that the six days in Genesis 1 are symbolic. St. Lawrence of Brindisi makes it clear that this verse is not the beginning of another account of Creation with an entirely different outlook but rather a development of what went before. He says: "It is very frequent in Sacred Scripture that a singular word is taken in place of a plural, which I think occurred here, such that "in the day" was written for "in the days.""

# DOCTRINE SEVEN

## God created the world
## several thousand years ago.

None of the Fathers of the Church believed in an ancient universe. From the writings of the Greek atomists they were familiar with the idea of the universe being formed over eons of time by natural forces, and they rejected it. The Church has not made a formal declaration about the age of the world. However, it is possible that she could someday declare that "yom" in Genesis 1 means a literal day because that interpretation has strong support in scriptural exegesis and in Tradition. That means that it is possible for her to formally teach that the world is only thousands of years old. However, she could never declare that "yom" means millions of years because that has no support at all in scriptural exegesis, Tradition, or magisterial teaching. The natural sciences are unable to say anything with certainty about the age of the world.

The exact age of the world cannot be determined from Scripture, but Scripture assures us that the world was created only thousands of years ago and surely not billions. The Bible gives the exact number of years from Creation to the death of Abraham, but unfortunately these numbers vary somewhat in variant texts. These texts, (Hebrew Masoretic, Greek Septuagint) give a range of roughly 1600-2400 years from Creation to the death of Abraham, for example. Using archeological evidence, most scholars agree that Abraham lived about 2000 BC. Taking all the variant text numbers into account, the world is at least 6,000 years old and at most 12,000 years old.

The variant texts do not destroy the credibility of the biblical chronology. The Church Fathers were aware of such discrepancies but were not greatly disturbed by them. They believed that the patriarchs lived to be hundreds of years old, the discrepancies notwithstanding. St. Augustine explicitly considers the question of "whether we should follow the authority of the Hebrew text rather than that of the Septuagint in the reckoning of the years." He says: "I should certainly not be justified in doubting that when some differences occur in the two versions, where it is impossible for both to be a true record of historical fact, then greater reliance should be placed on the original language from which a version was made by translators into another tongue." The Septuagint was a translation of the Hebrew Scriptures into Greek by a team of Jewish Scribes, between the third and second centuries BC. St. Augustine attributes the original deviation from the Hebrew text to a simple mistake by the scribe who first translated the text from Hebrew into Greek.

There are various chronologies calculating the age of the earth. One of the most famous is that by the Anglican Archbishop of Armagh, Ireland, James Ussher in about 1650. He calculated that Creation took place in 4004 BC. It was a 1,300 page work using the Masoretic and Septuagint texts. A Jewish Chronology based on the Seder Olan Rabbah was compiled in the 2nd century AD by Rabbi Yose ben Halafta and calculates the year of Creation as 3760 BC. The Eastern Orthodox chronologies, based on the Septuagint text, arrive at 5500 BC as the approximate year of Creation.

Many evolutionists calculate the age of the universe to be 10-20 billion years old, based on either measurements of radioactive elements in the rocks of the earth, or on the amount of time they believe it would take light to travel from the stars farthest away to earth and that the speed of light has remained constant over time. These issues will be discussed more, later on. Suffice it to say that estimating the earth's age involves a projection back in time of present day measurable conditions. It depends on assumptions about the constancy of certain factors over time, and initial and boundary conditions. Their calculations reject catastrophic events such as Noah's flood, while holding forth that geological and geophysical processes (presently operating) have remained largely unchanged throughout earth's history.

Even with a uniformitarian view of these processes, some phenomena still point to a young earth:

(1) Decay and reversal of the earth's magnetic field. This decay is related to an electric current circulating in the earth's core. The decay in the current is caused by electrical resistance. Extrapolating back in time, the current increases as does the heat it generates. Going back just 20,000 years the heat generated would have been enough to liquefy the earth. Reversal in the magnetic field could only be instigated by a catastrophic event like the Great Flood, thus pointing to an earth only thousands of years old.

(2) Helium content in the atmosphere. Helium is produced by radioactive decay inside the earth that rises to the surface and enters the atmosphere. Only a small amount escapes into space. Both the rate of introduction of helium into the atmosphere and that which escapes into space has been calculated. The concentration of helium present in the atmosphere has been measured. It is low, thus indicating a young earth.

(3) Delta formation. The Mississippi River pours about 300 million cubic yards of sediment into the Gulf of Mexico each year. At that rate, the Mississippi delta would have taken only about 4,000 years to form.

(4) Erosion and sedimentation. If the earth were billions of years old, current geological processes would have completely eroded it and filled the oceans with sediment. The surface of the earth, however, has suffered relatively little erosion, and the thickness of the sediment on the ocean floor indicates a much younger earth.

Some astronomical phenomena suggest that certain features of the universe are much younger than evolutionist science would suppose:

(1) Short period comets. The gradual destruction of many short period comets has been observed and recorded over the centuries. Their average lifespan is calculated at between 1,500 and 10,000 years. If the solar system was the same age as evolutionists say the earth is, namely 4.5 billion years old, the comets would long be gone, yet there are still many of them circling the sun and no new source of comets have been observed.

(2) Jupiter's volcanically active moon Io. NASA's Voyager mission revealed that Io is literally bubbling with volcanoes, and is the most volcanically active body in the solar system. Without an external source of thermal energy, Io should have cooled off a long time ago according to the evolutionary time scale. Fr. Warkulwiz also goes into other matters, such as Saturn's rings and lunar craters, both of which give evidence of a young age to the universe.

This is the point of these pivotal examples: Catholics must not allow themselves to be intimidated into abandoning biblical chronology and blindly accepting the speculations of modern astronomers concerning the age of the universe. The idea that the universe is ancient is not as scientifically certain as they claim. They interpret data and construct models with the preconceived notion that the universe is ancient, but there is significant scientific evidence that it is not. The facts of modern astronomy do not make it a necessity to "depart from the literal and obvious sense" in the interpretation of Genesis' chronology; quite the opposite, a correct interpretation of astronomical data agrees with the literal rendering of Genesis' chronology.

None of the Church Fathers believed in an ancient universe. They believed the earth was created in six natural days, except St. Augustine, who believed that everything was created at once. The Catechism (#223) says, "The question about the origins of the world and of man has been the object of many scientific studies which have splendidly enriched our knowledge of the age and dimensions of the cosmos, the development of life-forms and the appearance of man." Some see this as implied endorsement of the scientific opinion that the world is eons of years old because that is the opinion of the majority of present day scientists. But it is no such thing! It is a carefully worded statement of general remarks not endorsing any specific scientific opinion. It lauds genuine scientific knowledge, which can only be comprised of facts. That the cosmos is billions of years old is merely an opinion, not a fact, and a growing number of scientists do not agree with that opinion.

Fr. Warkulwiz lists four objections to the Church's teaching that the earth was created several thousand years ago. Two of them will be covered here, as parts of the others, such as the big bang theory, are covered elsewhere. The first objection is the assertion that radiometric measurements of rocks assure us that the earth is billions of years old. However, radiometric dating methods depend on belief in the assumptions employed and on data that are often conflicting. One method is Uranium-238 Radiometric Dating.

First of all this method, like all radiometric rock dating methods, applies only to igneous and metamorphic rocks. Igneous rocks were once extremely hot and molten and have cooled into solid rock, such as lava, basalt and deep granites. Metamorphic rock is rock that was transformed by heat or pressure, such as marble. Radiometric methods do not work on sedimentary rock, which is rock formed from the sediment laid down by water. Limestone, sandstone and shale are sedimentary rocks. Most fossils are buried in sedimentary rocks. Proponents of radiometric dating presume that the melting of a rock sets its radiometric clock to zero and that the age provided by the method is the time elapsed between the cooling of the rock and the present.

The first radioactive isotope used to date rocks was uranium-238. Through radioactive decay uranium-238 decays, (through a number of intermediate decays), to lead-206, which is stable. The half-life of the process is 4.5 billion years. That means that in 4.5 billion years half of the uranium-238 in a rock will have decayed into lead-206. So from a measure of the ratio of the amount of lead-206 to the amount of uranium-238 in a rock, the age of the rock can be determined IF (1) all the lead-206 came from uranium-238, that is, if there was no lead-206 in the rock to begin with, and IF (2) no uranium or lead entered or left the rock after it was formed, and IF (3) the decay rate, that is, the half-life, remained constant.

Now the *first* IF is an assumption about the initial condition of the rock. Is it justifiable to say that there was no lead-206 when the rock was formed? If lead-206 had been present, the method could give an age much older than the rock's true age. Also, does melting really set the clock to zero, eliminating all the lead-206? The *second* IF is an assumption about the boundary condition. Rocks are not as impermeable as one might suppose. Elements can enter or leave a rock in gaseous form or by leaching. Much care is taken in selecting rocks, but even the ages determined for good specimens are often inconsistent with the ages determined by other methods. For example, another radiometric method uses the decay of potassium-40 into argon-40. This method was used on rocks formed out of the molten lava from the eruption of Mount Saint Helens in 1980. It yielded ages measured in hundreds of thousands of years. This result indicates that the molten lava had not entirely degassed; that is, the clock was not set to zero.

Now let us consider the *third* IF, namely, the assumption about the constancy of the decay rate of uranium-238. Did the half-life of the uranium-238 remain constant from the time the rock was formed? It is known that the decay rate of some elements changes in the presence of a radiation environment. The following comments by three different scientists illustrate the problem: (1) "The age of our globe is thought to be some 4.5 billion years, based on the radio-decay rates of uranium and thorium. Such 'confirmation' may be short-lived, as nature is not to be discovered quite so easily. There has been in recent years the horrible realization that radio-decay rates are not as constant as previously thought, nor are they immune to environmental influences. And this could mean that the atomic clocks are reset during some global disaster, and events which brought the Mesozoic to a close may not be 65 million years ago but, rather, within the age and memory of man." (2) "In general, dates in the 'correct ballpark' are assumed to be correct and are published, but those in disagreement with other data are seldom published nor are discrepancies fully explained." (3) "It is obvious that radiometric techniques may not be the absolute dating methods that they are claimed to be. Age estimates on a given geological stratum by different radiometric methods are often quite different (sometimes by hundreds of millions of years.) There is no absolutely reliable long-term radiological 'clock'." Hovering about all these conventional assumptions is the overarching one that the earth is 4.5 billion years old, which evolutionists take as dogma, so the data must conform to that, or it is considered bad and, therefore, rejected.

Another objection to the teaching that the earth was created but a few thousand years ago is based upon the idea that Genesis' reference to the earth being "without form and void" may mean that this was a period of considerable length, from thousands to millions of years. Further, there are gaps in biblical genealogies, indicating that Scripture is giving an incomplete genealogical record and may instead be only giving lines of descent that may be very long. There is no hint in these first verses of Genesis that there are long periods of time there. For example, how could there have been matter for eons of time without light? There is an intimate relationship between matter and light, and light was clearly created on the first day. Christ Himself excluded any chronological gap in these verses. He identified "In the beginning" with Creation Week when He said, "But from the beginning of creation, 'God made them male and female.'" All things considered, the genealogical gaps and contradictions are not of great extent, and are at most in the order of several thousands of years, which do not disguise the "young-ness" of man and the universe. St Jerome, in his time, was aware of these problems but did not consider them serious enough for an exegete to spend much effort trying to resolve them.

# DOCTRINE EIGHT

## God created man in His image and likeness

The image of God is in man by imitation of the divine nature, which is intellectual and volitional, and also by imitation of divine person-hood. This is not so for brute animals, in which there is only a "trace" or "vestige" of the Creator. Therefore, man differs in essence from brute animals, and not only in degree. The Catechism frequently refers to Genesis 1:26-27 and the truth that man was created in the image of God. The doctrines connected with that truth are: 1) Man is able to know and love his Creator, [# 36, 356]; 2) Each man enjoys the dignity accorded a person [# 225, 337]; 3) God created everything for man [#299, 358]; 4) Man is called to a personal relationship with God [#299]; 5) Man is the summit of the Creator's work and distinguished among creatures [# 343]; 6) Man imitates the creative work of God Almighty, in his works of art [# 2501]; 7) Man was created crowned with glory and honor [#2809].

Genesis 1:26 states that God made man in His image and likeness. Verse 27 states that man was created in God's image but does not use the word likeness. The word "man" is used in verses 26-27 with a collective meaning; it means all human persons, not just Adam and Eve. Much has been written about the meaning of the words "image" and "likeness."

St Thomas Aquinas says that an image of something is both a likeness of the thing and a copy of it. He distinguishes likeness from image as follows: "Hence it is clear that likeness is essential to an image; that an image adds something to likeness—namely, that it is copied from something else. For an image is so called because it produces an imitation of something else; wherefore an egg, for instance, however much like and equal to another egg, is not called the image of the other egg, because it is not copied from it." He goes on to say: "Not every likeness, not even what is copied from something else, is sufficient to make an image; for if the likeness be only generic, or existing by virtue of some common accident, this does not suffice for one thing to be the image of another." He uses the example of a worm, even though it may emerge from a man's body, cannot be called the image of the man. And again he says, "Nor, if anything is made white like something else, can we say that it is the image of that thing; for whiteness is an accident belonging to many species. But the nature of an image requires likeness in species; thus the image of the king exists in his son . . ." He points out that likeness is both prior to image and subsequent to it. Likeness is prior to image because it is more general than image. Likeness is subsequent to image because it signifies a certain perfection of image. As Saint Augustine said, "For we say than an image is like or unlike what it represents, according as the representation is perfect or imperfect."

It is a metaphysical principle that every effect bears some likeness to its cause. The artist leaves "traces" of himself in his art. God is reflected in His creatures in the way that an artist is reflected in his art. St. Bonaventure expressed this truth by saying that the Trinity "shines forth" in creatures: ". . . the creation of the world is a kind of book in which the Trinity shines forth, is represented and found as the fabricator of the universe in three modes of expression, namely, in the modes of vestige, image and similitude, such that the reason for the vestige is found in all creatures; the reason for the image is in intelligent creatures or rational spirits alone; and the reason for similitude is in the Godlike only. Hence, as if by certain step-like levels, the human intellect is born to ascend by gradations to the supreme principle, which is God."

Every creature resembles its Creator to an extent depending on its perfections. The ontological perfections of being and goodness are common to all creatures. Every creature has a likeness to God in that it exists and is good. Man bears likeness to God in this sense. St. Thomas compares the "likeness to God" in man to the likeness of a man in a statue. Man is an "image of God" because in some way he "copies" Him. He goes on to say that man is an image of God not in the corporeal part of his nature but in the incorporeal part: "Man is said to be after the image of God, not as regards his body, but as regards that whereby he excels other animals . . . . Now man excels all animals by his reason and intelligence; hence it is according to his intelligence and reason, which are incorporeal, that man is said to be according to the image of God. But God made a spiritual image to Himself in man."

St Thomas further points out that the image of God is in man not only by imitation of the divine nature, which is an intellectual and volitional nature, but also by imitation of divine person-hood, which is possessed by each of the Three Persons of the Trinity. So man is an image of God as regards both nature and person-hood, which are distinct but closely related. The emphasis here will be placed on the latter because that is the least understood.

We get an intuitive grasp of the meaning of "person" through our own experience of "I". A man knows that he has a mind and a will, that his nature is that of a rational being. Yet the concept of person seems to be something super-added to that nature. We recognize ourselves to be persons even when the mind and the will are defective or inactive. We have a human nature, which is common with other human beings, and the person that one is acts through his own particular nature. Nature pertains to "what" one is; person pertains to "who" one is.

A person is an individual substance of an intelligent nature. A person is an "individual substance" because he exists in himself and not in anything else, nor is he a part of anything else. Individuality implies that person-hood is "incommunicable" because it cannot, like a nature, be shared. According to St. Thomas the very concept of a person excludes the idea of it being communicated to something else or of its being assumed by something else. Peter cannot be transformed into Paul, nor can the actions of Peter be the actions of Paul. Person-hood cannot be communicated from the whole to the part, for example, the person-hood of a man cannot be communicated to his brain alone. Nor is person-hood to be communicated from the individual to the universal. The species "man" is not a person. Besides incommunicability, there are other qualifiers that set off person-hood. They are the following: uniqueness (there is only one Peter), unrepeatability (there never was and never could be another Peter), indivisibility (there is no half Peter), and distinctiveness, (Peter is not Paul, is not Mary . . .). Other characteristics associated with a person, but which proceed from the intellectual and volitional nature united with a person, are self-knowledge and freedom of choice.

Here are some aspects of both Divine Person-hood and human person-hood:

Divine Person-hood: In Genesis 1:26 God says, "Let US make man in OUR image, after OUR likeness." Jewish and some early Christian writers interpreted the use of the personal plural to mean that God was addressing His heavenly court of angels. But the angels could not have helped, even in the fashioning of man's body, because the creation of the whole man from the earth was an act of special creation that could be done only by God. Others say that the plural is used to proclaim the greatness and power of God. However, the greater part of Catholic Tradition, in the light of the New Testament, sees the plural personal as referring to the Holy Trinity. The Church Fathers understood this verse to mean that the First Person of the Trinity was addressing the Second Person or the Second and Third Persons. Eventually, revelation of the mysteries of the Trinity and the Incarnation led the Church to make a clear distinction between person and nature. Lateran Council IV clearly defined that God is "indeed three Persons but one essence, substance, or nature entirely simple." The Councils of Ephesus (431) and Chalcedon (451) defined the dogma that Christ is a Divine Person with both a divine nature and a human nature. The third Council of Constantinople (680-81) held that Christ has both a divine will and a human will.

Human person-hood: St. Thomas identifies three ways in which the human person, through his intellectual nature, can imitate God by knowing and loving Him. In each of these ways man is an image of God. (1) The image of God is in man insofar as he has a natural aptitude for knowing and loving God. This was given to him when he was created. It is common to all men. (2) The image of God is in man, inasmuch as he actually and habitually knows and loves God, albeit imperfectly. This image was acquired when he was re-created in grace. This image is found only in the just. (3) The image of God is in man, insofar as he knows and loves God perfectly. This image consists in the "likeness" of glory. It is found only in the blessed.

Being an image of God does not make the human person an equal to God in any way. The human person is a limited but true image of God. St. Thomas makes the following comparison: "Man is called to the image of God, not that he is essentially an image, but that the image of God is impressed on his mind; as a coin is an image of a king, as having the image of the king." The intellect of man is infinitely weaker than the divine intellect, but man's mind still gives him great stature in creation because it enables him to participate in the life of God. Man is the only corporeal substance that is a person.

Man imitates God in that he is both capable of knowing and knows that he knows. His capacity to know leads him to seek truth. Man is an image of the Trinity in his ability to relate to other persons by knowing them, loving them and freely entering into friendship with them. Man imitates God's creative power in a finite way. He is able to freely fashion matter according to an image in his mind. In his arts, man produces images of God's creatures. Only the whole man, comprised of body and soul, is a person. The body is the principle of man's individuation, and the soul is the principle of a man's specific nature. The soul maintains the identity of the person through the myriad of changes undergone by the body. The special relationship of the soul to its body remains even after death. St. Thomas says that the soul "is established on the boundary line dividing corporeal from separate (angelic) substances."

The Catechism (#357) makes the connection between human person-hood and the image of God: "Being in the image of God the human individual possesses the dignity of a person, who is not just something, but someone. He is capable of self-knowledge, of self-possession and of freely giving himself and entering into communion with other persons. And he is called by grace to a covenant with his Creator, to offer him a response of faith and love that no other creature can give in his stead."

Man's person-hood gives him both rights and responsibilities. Being an image of God accords man a certain dignity that must be respected by other persons, and the liberty he possesses in having a free will is exercised with accountability both to God and to other human persons. He must act in accord with his dignity as an image of God. Moral law, which is both written on his conscience and taught to him, shows him how to do so. The Catechism (#356) gives the fundamental reason for the dignity of the human person: "Of all visible creatures only man is 'able to know and love his creator.' He is 'the only creature on earth that God has willed for its own sake,' and he alone is called to share, by knowledge and love, in God's own life. It was for this end that he was created, and this is the fundamental reason for his dignity."

Concerning person-hood, the "ontological" person is the person as such. The "empiriological" person is the ontological person as he manifests himself through his acts, powers and habits, all of which are accidents. Personality and character express the empiriological person. Personality expresses the person through non-moral acts. Character expresses the person through moral acts, that is, acts that have the quality of right and wrong. Person-hood is a gift. Personality and character are largely products of one's own acts. One can cultivate a personality or form a character, but one cannot cultivate or form person-hood. Personality is cultivated by the formation of physical, intellectual, and volitional habits. Character is formed by the acquisition of moral virtues. Personalities and characters vary from one individual to another. The phenomenon of multiple personalities affects only the empiriological person. The ontological person remains intact. That is, the same person takes on a number of personalities.

The phenomenon of consciousness (through the introspective analysis of the empiriological person) reveals the existence of the ontological person and the fact that the ontological person is something stable and enduring in the midst of change. Modern psychology for the most part has abandoned the concept of the ontological person and focuses exclusively on the empiriological person. Influenced by the doctrine of materialistic evolution, psychologists have reduced personhood to little more than states of consciousness, which they claim are epiphenomena of matter. Therefore, they are not getting right answers because they are asking the wrong questions, guided by a false paradigm.

# DOCTRINE NINE

## God created the first man
## immediately from the earth.

The Fathers and Doctors of the Church, indeed, and all of the popes, bishops and faithful for nineteen centuries believed that God created Adam immediately from the dust of the earth. This doctrine was unquestioned by Catholics until the twentieth century, with the onrush of evolutionary thinking. Materialistic, human evolution stands condemned by the mere fact that it eliminates the role of God in the origin of man. The Fourth Lateran Council and Vatican Council I both affirmed that God created man. The Provincial Council of Cologne (1860) condemned the notion of natural transformism, which states that natural processes alone prepared the body of a brute to receive a human soul. Pope Pius XII did allow the consideration of special transformism, in which God makes pre-existent living matter receptive to a human soul and infuses a human soul in it. But he did not allow it to be held as a proven fact because it presents serious theological problems. The notion of a progressive creation compromises the literal sense of Genesis, as this novelty is a concession to false opinion that various kinds of animals did not all appear on earth at once. The unearthings of anthropologists, when correctly interpreted, are in harmony with the Genesis account of the creation of man.

Adam's body was formed directly from the earth. That is the literal and obvious meaning of Genesis 2:7, and affirmed in 3:19, where Adam is reminded: "You are dust." The Catechism #362 says this is symbolic, but it is symbolic only in the sense that the word "dust" represents lifeless matter. For this was the belief of the Fathers and the Doctors of the Church. Whenever Scripture speaks of the origin of the human body, it identifies the source as dust or earth. Abraham testifies that he is "but dust and ashes." David said: "(He) remembers that we are dust." Sirach asks, "How can he who is dust and ashes be proud?" He further proclaims, "The Lord created man out of earth and turned him back to it again."

The Fathers often referred to God as fashioning Adam with his "hands" to show that God worked with pre-existent, nonliving matter. St. John Chrysostom said, "Do you see how things were created by a word? But let us see what it says afterward about the creation of man: 'And God shaped man.' (Gen. 2:7) See how, by means of condescension of terms employed for the sake of our weakness, it teaches at the same time both the manner of creation and its diversity or variety, so that, speaking in human terms, it indicates that man was shaped by the very hands of God, even as another Prophet says: 'Your hands created me and shaped me.'" (Job 10:8) St. Basil made it clear that God made man directly from the earth to distinguish him from the animals: "Above, the text says that God created; here it says how God created. If the verse had simply said that God created, you could have believed that he created (man) as he did for the beasts, for the wild animals, for the plants, for the grass. This is why, to avoid your placing him in the class of wild animals, the Divine word has made known the particular art which God has used for you: 'God took of the dust of the earth.'" St. Irenaeus, St. Cyril of Jerusalem, St. Gregory of Nyssa, St. Cyril of Alexandria, St. John Damascene, St. Ephrem, and others as well all expressed the same belief. God created Adam's body by transforming the accidental and substantial forms of existing matter. This is different from the way the bodies of his progeny would be formed. They would be formed by the process of generation, whereby living bodies give rise to living bodies of the same nature.

Genesis 2:7 says that God breathed into the nostrils of man the "breath of life," and "man became a living being." The Hebrew word translated "breath" is neshamah. The "breath of the Almighty" gave man a spiritual life in imitation of His own. It is the spiritual element in man that makes him what he is and gives him his unique dignity and a special place in the created world. Fathers of the Church sometimes speak of man as being composed of body, soul and spirit. St Augustine explains, "And while man consists of these three elements: spirit, soul and body, which sometimes are reckoned as two, for often the soul is included in the designation of spirit (for it is that certain rational part, which beasts do not have, that is called spirit), our chief element is the spirit."

St. John Damascene elaborates on the nature of man's soul. "The soul, then, is a living being, simple and incorporeal, invisible to the bodily eyes by its very nature, immortal, rational and intelligent; shapeless, making use of an organic body, to which body it imparts life, growth and feeling, and the faculty of generation; mind, being its purest part and in no way alien to it, for just as the eye is to the body, so is the mind to the soul. The soul enjoys free choice, having the faculty of willing and of acting, and it is changeable, which is to say, it is subject to change because it was created."

St. Thomas Aquinas wrote extensively on the soul. He says the soul is spiritual because it is independent of matter in its existence and, to some extent in its operations. The soul is not composed of matter. He says the soul is simple because there are no quantitative divisions in it. The soul is an indivisible entity. He says the soul is incorruptible because it has no quantitative parts to decompose, and it has powers that do not depend on matter. Finally, he says the soul is immortal because the only way it can be destroyed is through annihilation by God, but God will not do that because it would contradict His justice. Scholastic philosophy ascribes to the soul two spiritual dimensions, intellect and free will. Modern day philosopher Dietrich von Hildebrand adds the affections as a third dimension, as he considers this and other acts of the heart to be distinct from those of the intellect and will.

Plato taught that the soul and the body are distinct independent entities. He held that the soul is to the body as the pilot is to the ship. Aristotle held that the soul is the form of the living body, having a unique inseparable relationship with it. The Church Fathers and the Scholastics held a similar view to Aristotle, but, unlike Aristotle, they believed that the human soul could exist apart from the body. St John of Damascus held that the body and the soul were created simultaneously: "The body and the soul were formed at the same time—not one before the other . . . ." St Gregory of Nyssa professed the essential unity of man in arguing that the soul was not created for the sake of the body: "Nor are we again in our doctrine to begin by making up man like a clay figure and to say that the soul came into being for the sake of this, for surely in that case the intellectual nature would be shown to be less precious than the clay figure." The Scholastics taught that the body and the soul are substantially united. The soul is the substantial form of the body. This explains man's essential unity while retaining the distinction between the body and the soul. The human soul exists after death but as an incomplete substance. The Council of Vienne (1311-1312), Lateran Council V (1512-1517), and Pope Pius IX (1846-1878) affirmed that the rational soul is the essential form of the body. The Catechism (#362-368) devotes a whole section to the unity of the human person.

There are some today that claim that there is a striking discrepancy between the two accounts of the creation of man recorded in Genesis chapters 1 and 2. However if one examines them with the eyes of faith, rather than of skepticism, one finds that together these two form one consistent account. The narrative on the creation of man in Genesis 2 supplements that in Genesis 1. Genesis 1 relates the creation of creatures in the order of time while Genesis 2 relates them in order of significance. Man was the last creature created but is the one for whom all other creatures were created. When Genesis 2:19 says that God created every beast of the field and every bird and brought them to Adam it does not signify they were created after Adam but rather they were created for him. Eve's creation was not some type of afterthought as some maintain but that Adam was the first human and all other human beings, including Eve, proceeded from him. He is the prototype human being. Genesis 1:28 gives one reason for the creation of two kinds of human persons, namely, to be fruitful and multiply while Genesis 2:18 gives a second, namely, that Adam may have a human mate with complementary characteristics because his nature included a desire for such. These reasons are not contradictory but complementary.

Many people maintain that paleontological evidence shows that the human race evolved from inferior species, rather than man's being a special immediate creation directly from God as portrayed in Genesis. Darwin's view that man is descended from some lowly, organized form sparked the search for the so-called "missing link", the supposed transitional form between beast and man. In the "Descent of Man" Darwin erased the essential difference between man and animals: ". . . the difference in mind between man and the higher animals, great as it is, certainly is one of degree and not of kind." He compared similarities between man and beasts, especially the apes, and attempted to determine the origin and probable line of genealogy of the races of mankind. This is the philosophy that underlines modern physical anthropology, except that it no longer views the different human races as different species. Evolutionary anthropology "involves the discovery, analysis and description of fossilized human remains. Two key goals are the identification of the differences between the human and the human/nonhuman ancestors, and the clarification of the biological emergence of humankind." (Ency Brit) Collectively, modern humans, along with their human and nonhuman ancestors, are called hominids. These are the major hominids in the supposed evolutionary sequence leading up to modern man: (1) Australopithecus [southern ape] considered the oldest, some 4-million years by evolutionists; they are nonhuman creatures with a human-like morphology, from southern and eastern Africa. The most famous is called Lucy. (2) Homo habilis [dexterous man], in the genus homo, he is very primitive, allegedly 1.5-2.5 million years, from sub-Saharan Africa. He is depicted as walking on two feet and able to manipulate objects. Crude tools are found at the site. (3) Homo erectus [erect man] supposedly lived 250,000 to 1.6 million years ago in Africa, Asia, and Europe. The most famous are Java Man and Peking Man. (4) Homo sapiens [wise man], the genus to which modern man supposedly belongs, approximately 50 to 150 thousand years ago. Cro-Magnon Man is the most famous type, by far. (5) Neanderthal man, the first fossil of which is found in Germany's Neander Valley. He is listed separately, here, inasmuch as anthropologists continue to disagree on whether he is human or not. There is evidence that Neanderthals dwelt in caves; hunted animals; used fire, primitive tools and weapons; painted pictures; buried their dead and practiced a religion.

Paleoanthropology deals with fossil hominids. It is a field of great uncertainty and evolutionists themselves dub it the "bones of contention." It is an inexact science that begs the question by assuming that human evolution took place. Having gone "toe to toe" with reality, it then analyzes the data based on a postulate and concludes by saying the data confirm evolution! The dangers inherent in such a "methodology" can be seen in the case of the Piltdown Man hoax. Piltdown Man is the nomenclature given to pieces of an apparently fossilized human skull and ape-like lower jaw found between 1908 to1913 by Charles Dawson in a gravel pit near Lewes, England. Arthur Smith Woodward of the British Museum reconstructed the fossil fragments and proposed it as a new species of hominid, the missing link needed to complete evolutionary theory. The theory at that time predicted that the ancestor of human beings would have a large brain and an ape-like jaw. Woodward's reconstruction became widely accepted, at last, and it became the paradigm for interpretation of newly found fossils. This lasted for some forty years, until several fossils were found that didn't fit the paradigm. This led to Piltdown Man being exposed for what it was, an elaborate hoax. In 1953 several scientists proved that the skull belonged to a modern human and the jaw fragments to a modern orangutan. The jaw had been chemically treated to look like a fossil, and its teeth had been filed down to make them look human. It took four decades to discover the fraud because most scientists had accepted Woodward's assertion without question.

Science can be genuinely objective only when dealing with the present as there is much subjectivity in scientific reconstructions of the past. Despite popular conceptions to the contrary, australopithecines are but extinct primates that lived on earth at the same time as humans; and homo habilus is not valid, as it is constructed from two distinct fossil forms—a large human form and a smaller nonhuman form; Homo erectus and Neanderthal are both humans. Even so, a clear and comprehensive charting of the fossils shows that, as far back as the human fossil record goes, the human body has remained substantially the same and has not evolved from something else.

Artists and writers have been very skillful at depicting our imagined ancestors and giving them an aura of reality. This has provided evolutionists with a powerful propaganda tool. For example, *National Geographic* once commissioned four artists to reconstruct a female figure from the casts of seven fossil bones thought to be the same species as skull 1470. One artist drew a creature whose forehead is missing and whose jaws looked vaguely like those of a beaked dinosaur. The second drew a rather good looking modern African-American woman with unusually long arms. The third artist drew a somewhat scrawny female with arms like a gorilla and a face akin to that of a Hollywood werewolf. The fourth one drew a figure covered with body hair and climbing a tree, with beady eyes that glare out from under a heavy, gorilla-like brow. These drawings show clearly how a single set of fossils can be so differently reconstructed, from the mind's eye of an artist. Someone looking for an intermediate form to plug into an ape-to-human sequence could pick whatever drawing seems to fit best!

Materialistic evolutionism is the philosophy that holds that the whole man evolved into being through natural processes alone. Atheists adhere to it because God does not enter the picture. Agnostics and deists espouse it because God can be put so far into the background of the picture that it doesn't matter if He is really there or not. It is totally unacceptable to Catholics because it denies man a spiritual soul, thus contradicting Sacred Scripture, Tradition and defined doctrine. The Fourth Lateran Council and Vatican Council I declared that God created "the human, constituted as it were, alike of the spirit and the body." God created the body of the first man from existing matter and his soul directly from nothing.

When people lose contact with or reject the true account of human origins that is related in Genesis, something else fills the void. The denial of an essential difference between man and beast, which is the hallmark of materialistic evolutionism, has led to an aberrant new phenomenon; namely, animal rights activism. This movement carries evolutionism to its logical conclusion: since there is no essential difference between man and animals, it is said, animals have the same rights as men. In fact, they have a priority in rights over man because they were here first. The doctrine of evolution has become the philosophical foundation for practically all secularist thought. It has been applied beyond the origin of the universe, life and man. For example, evolution is said to be operative today on a societal level. This has given rise to some bizarre notions, such as the whole human species evolving into a single organism.

The evolution paradigm has even infected the thought of "Catholic" theologians and has been the cause of much fuzzy thinking in modern "Catholic" theology. The evolutionary fantasies dreamed up by Teilhard de Chardin are seen as profound spiritual insights by far too many Catholics. Theological modernism is deeply rooted in evolutionary soil. Many Christian and Catholic intellectuals have accepted the erroneous opinion that the fossil record demonstrates that life has been here on earth for millions of years and that life has advanced over those years to more and more complex forms. Trying to reconcile this view with Genesis they formulated the "day-age theory," which states that each of the six days of creation represents an immense period of time. One school of thought, theistic evolution, proposes that natural processes were predetermined, guided, or genetically programmed by God to produce this advance in life forms over long ages, but has no real evidence to support its theory. They hold that God created matter and that man has a soul. Cardinal Ruffini, writing in the 1950's, said that under this view an effect is produced that is superior to its cause: "And this is precisely the absurdity that the transformists meet when they assert that an animal was able to generate a body fit to be informed by a human soul, namely, with perfections superior to its own constitution and proper to a nature that is specifically diverse: because the human species is composed not only of a soul, but also of a body."

Another version of theistic human evolution says that God simultaneously transformed pre-existent, living matter into a human body and infused it with a specially created soul. Pope Pius XII allowed discussion and research along these lines but "this must be done in such a way that reasons for both opinions, that is, those favorable and those unfavorable to evolution be weighed and judged . . . and provided that all are prepared to submit to the judgment of the Church . . . ." He warned that: "Some however, rashly transgress this liberty of discussion, when they act as if the origin of the human body from pre-existing and living matter were already completely proved by the facts which have been discovered up to now . . . ."

A Catholic theistic evolutionist must also demonstrate that the theory of evolution he advocates is non-dualistic; that is, there is no replacement of a brute soul with a human soul, thereby treating the soul as if it were an independent complete substance, which would not be in conformity with Catholic teaching on the soul. The Catechism # 365 states: "The unity of soul and body is so profound that one has to consider the soul to be the 'form' of the body: i.e., it is because of its spiritual soul that the body made of matter becomes a living human body; spirit and matter, in man, are not two natures, united, but rather their union forms a single nature." In reality, the only way to avoid the taint of dualism is to admit the simultaneous creation of Adam's body and soul.

A third version of theistic evolution is known as progressive creation as exemplified in the late Fr. Patrick O'Connell's book "Science of Today and the Problems of Genesis" (1959). His effort to uphold the literal meaning of the Genesis account of Creation is hampered by his acceptance of long geological ages as scientific fact: "Our next conclusion is that a) as the fossils that appeared in the earliest geological stratum belonged to highly complicated and specialized organisms, b) that as organisms have continued unchanged for hundreds of millions of years, and c) that as fossils of multitudes of new organisms unconnected with those that have gone before them have appeared suddenly on the earth just at times when it was in a fit state to receive them, the account given in Genesis best explains these facts that science has discovered."

This is form of progressive creation, i.e., God intervening at certain times in the history of the planet to create new species, does not conform to Genesis, as Fr. O'Connell portrays the six days of Creation in terms of eons of time. While the Pontifical Biblical Commission in 1909 allowed the word yom to be interpreted as a "certain space of time" turning that phrase into millions of years is quite a stretch of the imagination. Even granting that interpretation, one still cannot conform progressive creation to Genesis because the fossil sequence of supposed successive-creations does not agree with the Genesis sequence. We don't find only plants (created on Day Three) in the "oldest" layer and only water creatures and birds (created on Day Five) in the next level, and so on. Also, living creatures closely depend on each other; for but one example, there is the interdependence of bees, flowers and plants in the pollination process. Could each of these three exist millions of years awaiting the appearance of the others? Thus the author compromises the literal sense of Genesis, though his assessment of the age of the human species of some 12-22 thousand years is in the biblical ballpark.

# DOCTRINE TEN

## God created the first woman immediately from the body of the first man.

The Fathers of Holy Church believed the Genesis account of the creation of Eve literally, although they sometimes imposed allegorical interpretations on it. The creation of Eve from the side of Adam is so strongly affirmed in magisterial teaching that it can be considered as having been proposed infallibly by the universal and ordinary Magisterium of the Church. The firmness of the doctrine of the special creation of Eve's body strengthens the case against the evolution of Adam's body. For if Adam's body evolved, then Eve would have had a much nobler origin than Adam, God having created her directly and Adam through innumerable secondary causes. There would have then been an unthinkable disparity in dignity between the first man and the first woman.

Genesis 2:18-25 tells of the creation of the first woman, Eve. It begins with God saying: "It is not good that man should be alone. I will make him a helper fit for him." By saying "not good" God meant that His creation was not yet complete. Adam finds himself alone in the garden that God had planted for him to cultivate (Gen. 2:8-17). God sees that Adam is alone despite the fact that Adam has a personal relationship with God Himself. God made the man a part of creation and put into his condition a need for other creatures and in his nature a desire for communion with other creatures. God first brings animals to Adam to show him that they can be helpers and of service to him, and Adam gives them names expressive of their respective natures. The animals were created for man (Catechism # 2417).

St. Ephrem the Syrian makes note of the perfect harmony that existed between Adam and the animals: "Moses said, 'God brought them to Adam.' This happened that God might make known the wisdom of Adam and the harmony that existed between the animals and Adam before he transgressed the commandment. The animals came to Adam as to a loving shepherd. Without fear they passed before him in orderly fashion, by kinds and species. They were neither afraid of him nor were they afraid of each other." Even though the animals lived in perfect harmony with Adam and could be his helpers, they could not be his intimate companions. For Adam had discovered that he was essentially different from the animals and all other creatures.

Pope John Paul II said that the meaning of Adam's original solitude had two meanings: ". . . one derived from man's very nature, that is, from his humanity, and the other derived from the male-female relationship." The first meaning is based on Adam's awareness of his superiority among creatures. He is also different because he has self knowledge, as Pope John Paul continues, "Self-knowledge develops at the same rate as knowledge of the world, of all the visible creatures, of all the living beings to which man has given a name to affirm his own dissimilarity with regard to them. In this way consciousness reveals man as the one who possesses a cognitive faculty as regards the visible world. With this knowledge which, in a certain way, brings him out of his own being, man at the same time reveals himself to himself in all the peculiarity of his being. He is not only essentially and subjectively alone. Solitude also signifies man's subjectivity, which is constituted through self-knowledge. Man is alone because he is 'different' from the visible world, from the world of living beings." The Pope goes on to point out, "At the same time he (Adam) asserts himself as a 'person' in the visible world." The second meaning of Adam's solitude, according to the Pope, is contained in his expectation of a communion of persons: ". . . man's solitude is presented to us not only as the first discovery of the characteristic transcendence peculiar to the person. It is also presented as the discovery of an adequate relationship 'to' the person, and therefore as an opening and expectation of a 'communion of persons.'"

Genesis 2:21-22 tells of the creation of Eve from the rib of Adam: "So the Lord caused a deep sleep to fall upon the man, and while he slept took one of his ribs and closed up its place with flesh; and the rib which the Lord God had taken from the man he made into a woman and brought her to the man." The Church Fathers generally understood this account of the creation of Eve in the literal sense, but they also read it in an allegorical sense as well. For example, St. Augustine said: "Now in creating woman at the outset of the human race, by taking a rib from the side of the sleeping man, the Creator must have intended, by this act, a prophecy of Christ and his Church. The sleep of that man clearly stood for the death of Christ; and Christ's side, as he hung lifeless on the cross, was pierced by a lance. And from the wound there flowed blood and water, (Jn 19:34) which we recognize as the sacraments by which the Church is built up. This, in fact, is the precise word used in Scripture of woman's creation; it says not that God 'formed', or 'fashioned' a woman but that 'He built it (the rib) up into a woman' (Gn. 2:22). Hence the Apostle also speaks of the 'building up' of the body of Christ, which is the Church. (Eph. 4:12) The woman, then, is the creation of God, just as is the man; but her creation out of man emphasizes the idea of the unity between them; and in the manner of that creation there is, as I have said, a foreshadowing of Christ and his Church." And St. Cyril of Jerusalem connects the creation of Eve with the virgin birth of Christ: "Of whom in the beginning was Eve begotten? What mother conceived her, the motherless? But the Scripture says she was born out of Adam's side. Is Eve then born out of man's side without a mother, and is a child not to be born without a father, of a virgin's womb? This debt of gratitude was due to men from womankind: for Eve was begotten of Adam and not conceived of a mother, but as it were brought forth of man alone."

The creation of Eve from the side of Adam is well attested to in magisterial teaching. Pope Pelagius I solemnly taught that the first woman was created "from the rib of man." Pope Leo XIII strongly affirmed it against revilers, saying: "The revilers of the Christian faith refuse to acknowledge the never-interrupted doctrine of the Church on this subject, and have long striven to destroy the testimony of all nations of all times; they have nevertheless failed not only to quench the powerful light of truth, but even to lessen it. We record what is to all known, and cannot be doubted by any, that God, on the sixth day of creation, having made man from the slime of the earth, and having breathed into his face the breath of life, gave him a companion, whom He miraculously took from the side of Adam when he was locked in sleep. God thus, in His most far-reaching foresight, decreed that this husband and wife should be the natural beginning of the human race, from whom it might be propagated and preserved by an unfailing fruitfulness throughout all futurity of time." And the Catechism # 371 says, "God created man and woman together and willed each for the other. The Word of God gives us to understand this through various features of the sacred text. 'It is not good that man should be alone. I will make a fit helper for him' (Gn. 2:18). None of the animals can be man's partner (Gn. 2:19-20). The woman God 'fashions' from the man's rib and brings to him elicits on the man's part a cry of wonder, an exclamation of love and communion: 'This at last is bone of my bones and flesh of my flesh' (Gn. 2:23). Man discovers woman as another 'I, sharing the same humanity."

Genesis makes it clear that Eve shared not only Adam's nature but also his flesh. This implies that Eve received all of her chromosomes from Adam. She was genetically the same as Adam except for sexual differences. She was the female twin of Adam. Adam had one X and one Y chromosome. God gave Eve two of Adam's X chromosomes but no Y chromosome. A similar event would happen again in the future. The Word Incarnate would become the male twin of His mother because He received all of His chromosomes from her. In that case God transformed one of Mary's X chromosomes into a Y chromosome. All genetic properties trace back to Adam. Eve did not contribute any new genetic information. Adam possessed all the seed for the entire human species. This does not detract from the dignity of Eve. Rather it makes her one with Adam. This is another way the human species differs from animal species. The animals were created male and female simultaneously, and therefore the genetic information was divided between both sexes.

St. Ambrose said that God created Eve from the body of Adam to assure the unity of the human species, to eliminate the possibility that disparate natures should arise: "Nor is it a matter of indifference that the woman was not formed of the same clay from which Adam was made, but was made from the rib of Adam himself, so that we might know that the flesh of man and woman is of but one nature, and that there is but one source of the human race. Therefore at the beginning it is not two that are made, man and woman, nor two men, nor two women, but first man is made, and then woman from him. For God willed to settle one nature upon mankind, and starting from the one origin of this creature, He snatched away the possibility of numerous and disparate natures."

St. Thomas Aquinas gave four reasons why it was suitable for the woman to be made from the man: "a) to give the first man a certain dignity consisting in this, that as God is the principle of the whole universe, so the first man, in likeness to God, was the principle of the whole human race; b) that man might love woman all the more, and cleave to her more closely, knowing her to be fashioned from himself; c) because . . . the human male and female are united, not only for generation, as with other animals, but also for the purpose of domestic life, in which each has his or her particular duty, and in which the man is head of the woman; d) there is a sacramental reason for this; for by this is signified that the Church takes her origin from Christ."

The Catechism # 369 emphasizes the equal dignity of the two sexes: "Man and woman have been created, which is to say, willed by God: on the one hand, in perfect equality as human persons; on the other, in their respective beings as man and woman. 'Being man' or 'being woman' is a reality which is good and willed by God: man and woman possess an inalienable dignity which comes to them immediately from God their Creator (Gn. 2:7, 22). Man and woman are both with one and the same dignity 'in the image of God.' In their 'being-man' and 'being-woman,' they reflect the Creator's wisdom and goodness."

The union of the sexes continues God's plan of creation through procreation. Man and woman imitate "in the flesh the Creator's generosity and fecundity" (CCC # 2335) by bringing children into the world and raising them. And Catechism # 372 says, "God unites them in such a way that, by forming 'one flesh' they can transmit human life." The mutual love of spouses "becomes an image of the absolute and unfailing love with which God loves man." (CCC # 1604) Jesus recalled Gn. 1:27-28 and 2:24 when He affirmed the institution and indissolubility of the conjugal union between a man and a woman, which was first established with Adam and Eve: "Have you not read that he who made them from the beginning made them male and female, and said, 'For this reason a man shall leave his father and mother and be joined to his wife, and the two shall become one?' So they are no longer two but one. What therefore God has joined together, let no man put asunder."

Some of the Church Fathers believed that if there were no Fall, human reproduction would have been accomplished by means other than sexual intercourse. St. Augustine originally held that view but later came to the view that sexual union was part of God's plan. St. Thomas said that there would have been generation in the state of innocence for the multiplication of individuals in the human species: "In the state of innocence there would have been generation of offspring for the multiplication of the human race; otherwise man's sin would have been very necessary, for such a great blessing to be its result . . . . Hence it belongs to man to beget offspring, on the part of the naturally corruptible body. But on the part of the soul, which is incorruptible, it is fitting that the multitude of individuals should be the direct purpose of nature, or rather of the Author of nature, Who alone is the Creator of the human soul. Wherefore, to provide for the multiplication of the human race, He established the begetting of offspring even in the state of innocence." He further points out that even though, in the state of innocence, generation would not be required to preserve the species, it would still be needed for the multiplication of individuals. And, "God made man and woman before sin. But nothing is void in God's works. Therefore, even if man had not sinned, there would have been such intercourse, to which the distinction of sex is made."

The great twentieth century philosopher Dietrich von Hildebrand observed that man and woman are "two different expressions of human nature." Their difference "has a specifically complementary character." Man and woman are "spiritually ordered toward each other," and "a much closer communion and ultimate love is possible between them than persons of the same sex because of their complementary difference."

Von Hildebrand said that it is not possible to overemphasize the fact "that the difference between man and woman is not merely a biological one, but extends to the deep realm of personality." Love between a man and a woman engenders a unique "I-thou communion," an intense longing for union, and blissful enchantment, with the spouse "fully seen as person." Happiness is love's outcome, but never its motive. The happiness of the beloved is of very special importance. Love is so focused on the unique person, "who can never be replaced by another. If it were possible to conceive of someone who perfectly duplicated another person's potential and value in every way—something which is altogether untenable—one of the two would still be the one loved and there would never be a desire to exchange him for the other."

Pope John Paul II makes the point that man is an image of God not only through his intelligence and dominion over nature but also in the communion between the male and the female versions of the human person: ". . . man became the 'image and likeness' of God not only through his own humanity, but also through the communion of persons which man and woman form right from the beginning. The function of the image is to reflect the one who is the model, to reproduce its own prototype. Man becomes the image of God not so much in the moment of solitude as in the moment of communion. Right 'from the beginning' he is not only an image in which the solitude of a person who rules the world is reflected, but also, and essentially, an image of inscrutable divine communion of persons."

One objection to this teaching is that genetics has shown that the first woman lived in Africa about 200,000 years ago. According to this objection, science has shown that the biblical chronology, which gives the first woman an age under 10,000 years, is way off the mark. This particular objection is somewhat dated, but it is pertinent because it is a glaring example of how bad science is popularized and is used to discredit religion. The genetics referred to in the objection is contained in the so-called mitochondrial Eve theory.

The mitochondrion is a site in a living human cell at which metabolic activities take place that produce energy for the body. It carries its own DNA, labeled mtDNA, which is in addition to the DNA in the nucleus of the cell. Mitochondrial DNA has been called a biological history book of women because it is passed on from generation to generation only by mothers, unlike nuclear DNA, which is passed on by both parents. In 1987, three California biochemists proposed a new way of tracing human origins using mtDNA. The basic assumption they made is that everyone in the world would have identical mtDNA if it were not for occasional mutations. But mutations do happen, and each mutation establishes a new mitochondrial "family." Those with the same mtDNA descended from the same mother. By tracing all the families back, one could arrive at the original ancestor. The inventors of the method assumed that there was no mixing of families from generation to generation, that all the changes in mtDNA were the result of mutations, and that these mutations occurred at a constant rate. They studied 136 women of various races from around the world. Their analysis led back to a single ancestral mtDNA molecule from a woman living in Africa about 200,000 years ago.

The theory is based on evolution and is subject to severe criticism on several counts. First, it looks for the family tree with the least number of mutational changes based on the assumption that evolution would have taken the most direct and efficient path—a strange thing for a random process to achieve! A statistical analysis showed that the 136 mtDNA sequences studied could result in more than a billion such family trees. Also, the computer program they used was very sensitive to the order in which the data was fed into it, which affected the place of origin of "Eve." One geneticist suggested that low-level mixing among early human populations may have scrambled the DNA sequences enough to make the method completely ineffective for locating and dating "Eve." One of the original researchers acknowledged that the African Eve has been invalidated. Marvin Lubenow (an opponent of mtDNA presumptions) critiques the theory for its evolutionary assumptions and its claims to be an independent confirmation of evolution: "The mtDNA study of African Eve, as well as other aspects of molecular genetics, is based on mutations in the DNA nucleotides. Perhaps we could be forgiven for asking the question, When an evolutionist looks at human DNA nucleotides, how does he know which ones are the result of mutations and which ones have remained unchanged? Obviously, to answer that question he must know what the original or ancient sequences were. Since only God is omniscient, how does the evolutionist get the information about those sequences that he believes existed millions of years ago? He uses as his guide the DNA of the chimpanzee. In other words, the studies that seek to prove that human DNA evolved from chimp DNA start with the assumption that chimp DNA represents the original condition (or close to it) from which human DNA diverged. This is circularity with a vengeance."

Lubenow continues with an examination of the method by which the "molecular clock" is calibrated. Since there is nothing in the mtDNA molecules that indicate how often they mutate, an outside standard must be used. The standard used is the mutation rate of various species whose divergence or evolution is determined from the dates assigned to fossils. This method made "Eve" 200,000 years old. He concludes: "Hence, an evolutionary time scale obtained from an evolutionary interpretation of fossils was superimposed upon the DNA molecules. Once again, the circularity is obvious. The alleged evidence for evolution from the DNA molecules is not an independent confirmation of evolution but is instead based upon an evolutionary interpretation of fossils as its starting point."

# DOCTRINE ELEVEN

## God gave man dominion over all creation.

Sacred Scripture makes it clear that God made everything for man. This was the belief of the Fathers and the Doctors of the Church and is affirmed by the Catechism of the Catholic Church. Genesis relates that God built the universe around man's home, earth; and modern astrophysical observations indicate that the earth occupies a central position in the universe. The attempt to dethrone man and proclaim his insignificance in the cosmos is not a gesture of humility, but one of infidelity.

The world was created to the glory of God. But God created everything for the sake of mankind. Man is the only creature on earth that God willed for its own sake—see Catechism # 356. He created all other creatures for the good of man, into whose custody He placed them. Man in return was (Catechism # 358) "to serve and love God and to offer all creation back to him." The offering back to God from the gifts of creation is the raison d'etre of ritual sacrifice. Man's dominion over the world proceeds from his being an image of God. God is the Lord of creation, and He made His image, man, to stand in for Him as the lord steward of creation.

Vatican Council II commented on man's work of subduing the earth and perfecting the work of creation: "By the work of his hands and with the aid of technical means man tills the earth to bring forth fruit and make it a dwelling place fit for all mankind; he also consciously plays his part in the life of social groups; in so doing he is realizing the design, which God revealed at the beginning of time, to subdue the earth (Gn. 1:28) and perfect the work of creation, and at the same time he is improving his own person: he is also observing the command of Christ to devote himself to the service of his fellow men." That God called man to "perfect the work of creation" does not mean that the world was defective in any way. It just means that God left it unfinished so that man might share in His work.

Pope John Paul II recalls Scripture verses that extol the dominion given to man: "The biblical text clearly shows the breadth and the depth of the lordship which God bestows on man. It is a matter first of all of dominion over the earth and over every living creature, as the Book of Wisdom makes clear: 'O God of my fathers and Lord of mercy . . . by your wisdom you have formed man, to have dominion over the creatures you have made, and rule the world in holiness and righteousness' (Wis. 9:1, 2-3). The Psalmist too extols the dominion given to man as a sign of glory and honor from his Creator: 'You have given him dominion over the works of your hands; you have put all things under his feet, all sheep and oxen, and also the beasts of the field, the birds of the air, and the fish of the sea, whatever passes along the paths of the sea'" (Ps. 8:6-8). The Pope continues by pointing out that man's dominion is not absolute and requires responsible stewardship. He also explains that the prohibition "but of the tree of the knowledge of good and evil you shall not eat" (Gen 2:17) showed that man was subject to moral laws as well as natural laws. It also shows that only God has absolute dominion over the world.

In the Fourth Eucharistic Prayer of the Roman Missal, which summarizes salvation history, God is praised for His wisdom and love in setting man over creation: "Father, we acknowledge your greatness: all your actions show your wisdom and love. You formed man in your own likeness and set him over the whole world to serve you, his creator, and to rule over all creatures." Man's rule is fourfold: over himself, over other men, over animals, over inanimate creatures. Man's primary mastery is over himself, as Catechism # 377 makes clear: "The 'mastery' over the world that God offered man from the beginning was realized above all within man himself: mastery of self. The first man was unimpaired and ordered in his whole being because he was free from the triple concupiscence (Cf. Jn 2:16) that subjugates him to the pleasures of the senses, covetousness for earthly goods, and self-assertion, contrary to the dictates of reason."

Even if there had been no Fall, government would still be needed in order to maintain an orderly society. In the state of innocence all men would have been without defects but not equal in all ways, as Aquinas indicates: "We must needs admit that in the primitive state there would have been some inequality, at least as regards sex, because generation depends upon diversity of sex; and likewise as regards age; for some would have been born of others; nor would sexual union have been sterile." Moreover, as regards the soul there would have been inequality as to righteousness and knowledge. Some would have made greater progress in virtue and knowledge than others; while some men would have been masters over others, ideally becoming servants advancing the common good.

Animals differ essentially from man. Man is master over the animals because he is superior to them, not in degree but in nature. The animal nature is between that of machine and man, just as man's nature is between that of animal and angel. Although many characteristics of animals are ordered toward the preservation of the individual or species, it is not for their own sake that they are being preserved; it is for man's sake. Animals have no rights [save for biblical ideas of freedom from cruelty, at the hands of man? *ed.*] because they are not persons; they were not created in the image and likeness of God. Some of the obvious signs of this are the following: they do not have a language; they do not invent; they do not have a sense of humor; they show no appreciation for the true, the good, or the beautiful. Animal behavior mimics man's behavior; intelligence, emotions, even expressions of pain, may be mimicked. But their behavior is totally instinctive, not reflective. That is why there is no bad behavior by animals. They cannot make moral choices. Even the use of tools, the ability to adapt behavior, and the ability to communicate with humans are instinctive and not the result of invention and free choices. Animal behavior is not the result of evolution, not the result of natural selection in the struggle for survival. It is the result of instincts God wired into animals so that they may achieve their ends, which are ultimately for the benefit of man.

Adam may have had a greater knowledge of the inner life of animals than we do, but if he did it was lost in the Fall. And much of his control of animals was certainly lost. Some saints, like Francis of Assisi, were given the gift of an Adam-like intimacy with animals. St. Augustine made the point that even though man may have lost some control over the animals after the Fall, he remains the master: "At times the Manicheans also ask, 'In what sense did man receive power over the fish of the sea and the birds of heaven and all the cattle and wild animals? For we see that men are killed by many wild animals and that many birds harm us when we want to avoid them or capture them, though we often cannot. In what sense then did we receive power over these?' On this point they should first be told that they make a big mistake when they consider man after sin, when he has been condemned to the mortality of this life and has lost that perfection by which he was made in the image of God. But even man's state of condemnation involves such power that he rules many animals. For though he can be killed by many wild animals on account of the fragility of his body, he can be tamed by none, although he tames very many and nearly all of them."

St. Thomas Aquinas believed that when man was in the state of innocence no animal disobeyed him; but because of his disobedience to God, he was punished by the disobedience of animals: "for his disobedience to God, man was punished by the disobedience of those creatures which should be subject to him. Therefore in the state of innocence, before man had disobeyed, nothing disobeyed him that was naturally subject to him." He further argued that the nature of animals did not change with man's sin. There were predators and prey before the Fall, just as there are after. But no animal, including those that were not tame, would have been exempted from the mastership of man. All animals would have obeyed man of their own accord, through their natural instinct, as today some domestic animals obey him. Man was given mastership over all material creatures, even inanimate ones by his use of them.

Genesis says that man was given dominion over the earth, but it says nothing about dominion over the universe. Man is not able to exercise dominion over the whole universe, but still the whole universe was made for his sake, in ways known to us—to provide light, heat and temporal rhythms, to provide reference points for navigation, to inspire awe and to manifest the glory of God—and in ways unknown to us. Scripture confirms this where it says that God created the sun and the moon and the stars "for signs and for seasons, and for days and years" (Gn. 1:14) and for the service of the nations. St. Bonaventure said that God created the universe for man so that man may use created things to ascend to loving and praising Him. And the Catechism # 2293 hails scientific and technological research as an expression of man's dominion over nature, but that this will not supply the answers to all questions important to man: "Basic scientific research, as well as applied research, is a significant expression of man's dominion over creation. Science and technology are precious resources when placed at the service of man and promote his integral development for the benefit of all. By themselves however they cannot disclose the meaning of existence and of human progress . . . ."

Genesis makes it clear that man and his home, earth, are the focus of the universe. Pope John Paul II, speaking to a group of scientists, affirmed this: "By increasing his knowledge of the universe, and in particular of the human being, who is at its center, man has a veiled perception, as it were, of the presence of God, a presence which he is able to discern in the 'silent manuscript' written by the Creator in creation, the reflection of his glory and grandeur." This view was well accepted by medieval men, scientists and poets alike. The theological confusion caused by Galileo's aggressive advocacy of heliocentric astronomy had the sad effect of clouding the truth of man's centrality and shattering the medieval vision.

Cardinal Bellarmine eloquently upheld that vision: "To demonstrate that the appearances are saved by assuming the sun at the center and the earth in the heavens is not the same thing as to demonstrate that in fact the sun is in the centre and the earth in the heavens. I believe that the first demonstration may exist, but I have very grave doubts about the second; and in case of doubt one may not abandon the Holy Scriptures as expounded by the holy Fathers . . ." Bellarmine's judgment was penetrating. It reached the heart of the issue. The sun-centered system did prove very useful in describing the motions of the planets relative to the sun and each other. But it has never been proven, nor can it be proven that the sun is at absolute rest with the earth and the other planets in absolute motion around it. In fact, according to Albert Einstein, statements about the absolute motion of the earth and sun are meaningless because it is possible to eliminate the notion of absolute motion from physics. One is free to choose the earth at rest or the sun at rest; it is simply a matter of convenience. Genesis 1 states that God created the earth first and built the rest of the universe around it. Nothing that modern science can demonstrate gives an account for the origin of motion in the universe.

There is evidence from modern astronomy that our galaxy is at the center of the universe. It is summarized by Russell Humphreys: "Over the last few decades, new evidence has surfaced that restores man to a central place in God's universe. Astronomers have confirmed that numerical values of galaxy redshifts are 'quantitized', tending to fall into distinct groups. According to Hubble's law, redshifts are proportional to the distances of the galaxies from us. Then it would be the distances themselves that fall into groups. That would mean the galaxies tend to be grouped into (conceptual) spherical shells concentric around our home galaxy, the Milky Way."

In contrast to the medievals, the modern view adhered to by many scientists and scholars today was clearly expressed by Bertrand Russell: "That man is the product of causes which had no prevision of the end they were achieving; that his origin, his growth, his hopes and fears, his loves and his beliefs, are but outcomes of the accidental collocations of atoms; that no fire, no heroism, no intensity of thought and feeling, can preserve an individual life beyond the grave; that all the labours of the ages, all the devotion, all the inspirations, all the noonday brightness of human genius, are destined to extinction in the vast death of the solar system, and that the whole temple of Man's achievement must inevitably be buried beneath the debris of a universe in ruins—all these things, if not quite beyond dispute, are yet so nearly certain, that no philosophy which rejects them can hope to stand. Only within the scaffolding of these truths, only on the firm foundation of unyielding despair, can the soul's habitation henceforth be safely built." What a dismal philosophy! Yet this is constantly what we are being told by scientists, by the communications media, and by other opinion makers. We are told that we are being egocentric when we assert that man is the center of the world; we are told that we humans are just inconsequential specks in the vastness of the universe, that there are probably many more species out there more intelligent and virtuous than us. But actually the egocentricity is on the side of those who so sanctimoniously deprecate man. They smugly set aside the truth in the Word of God to worship their own thoughts. In the medieval view nature is subservient to man; in the modern view man is the product of nature.

Philosophers of science have created a whole new lexicon for modern metaphysics and cosmology that does not contain the terms of the Scholastics. The Schoolmen thought in terms of substance, accident, essence, matter, form, actuality and potentiality. Modern philosophers think only in terms of space, time and energy/matter. The first two had little importance for the medieval philosophers. For them space and time were accidental and not self-subsistent. Instead, they thought of the ongoing passage of potentiality into actuality. Further, modern science looks for efficient causes, the how of things. The medieval scientist looked for final causes, the why of things—the why of material things in terms of their usefulness to men and the why of man in terms of his relationship with God. The time is right for a return to the medieval view, not unaltered but enhanced by authentic discoveries of the natural sciences. The restoration will follow a return to the correct understanding of Genesis. Pope John Paul implored scientists to recognize this: "Faith for its part is able to integrate and assimilate every research, for all research, through a deeper understanding of created reality and all its specificity, gives man the possibility of discovering the Creator, the source and goal of all things."

Now that the modern worldview has dethroned man from his unique place in creation, men have begun to look elsewhere in the universe for intelligent life. Evolutionists apply themselves to the search with religious fervor. They believe that life evolved here and therefore could also have evolved elsewhere. But despite several decades of intense looking, searchers for extraterrestrial life have not seen any sign of life out there, intelligent or otherwise. The failure to find intelligent life is called the Fermi Paradox after the Italian physicist Enrico Fermi who asked the famous question, "Where is everybody?" This was a response to the belief that, considering the supposed size and age of the universe, extraterrestrial civilizations must exist, and some should have made themselves known to us by now. The believers in extraterrestrial life find themselves in the awkward position of having to contrive reasons to explain why there is no evidence for their belief. In reality there is no compelling evidence for the existence of intelligent creatures in the universe besides human beings on earth.

Is it reasonable for a Catholic to believe that there are other personal corporeal substances in the universe, a la Star Wars and Star Trek? It seems not, because such an idea opens the door to the notion of multiple incarnations. If the Second Person of the Blessed Trinity united His Divine nature with a human nature, why couldn't He do so with other intelligent corporeal natures if they existed? The reason He couldn't is because the union between Christ's two natures is so complete that it demands uniqueness if it is not to contradict itself. The very essence of the union excludes any additional unions with other rational corporeal natures, as if the Word were the Hindu god Vishnu with his various avatars. Consider that Jesus Christ is an individual substance and that each such union would also be an individual substance, but all would be the same Person! So the idea that the Word of God would have multiple incarnations is as senseless as the idea of a human being sharing his person-hood among a number of human bodies. Or, if there were other rational corporeal natures, and He took on only one of them, why would he have taken on a human nature rather than some other? St. Paul affirmed the uniqueness of Christ. For he wrote that it was Christ whom God sent "to reconcile to himself all things, whether on earth or in heaven, making peace by the blood of his cross."

St. Peter Chrysologus eloquently sums up the eminence of man in creation: "Why then, man, are you so worthless in your own eyes and yet so precious to God? Why render yourself such dishonor when you are honored by him? Why do you ask how you were created and do not seek to know why you were made? Was not this entire visible universe made for your dwelling? It was for you that the light dispelled the overwhelming gloom; for your sake was the night regulated and the day measured; and for you were the heavens embellished with the varying brilliance of the sun, the moon and the stars. The earth was adorned with flowers, groves and fruit; and the constant marvelous variety of lovely living things was created in the air, the fields, and the seas for you, lest sad solitude destroy the joy of God's new creation. And the Creator still works to devise new things that can add to your glory. He has made you in his image that you might in your person make the invisible Creator present on earth; he has made you his legate, so that the vast empire of the world might have the Lord's representative." St Peter Chrysologus says further that God did much more than place His image as representative in the world. In Jesus Christ God fully revealed Himself in man, His creature, not merely as an image but in reality. The Creator brought great dignity to the human species by manifesting Himself in the man Jesus Christ. This He did without any loss of His own dignity.

# DOCTRINE TWELVE

## God created the first man and woman in a state of happiness and innocence.

According to Scripture and Tradition, God created the first human beings with many unspoiled natural gifts and with the preternatural gifts of freedom from suffering, infused knowledge, absence of concupiscence, and bodily immortality. The Church has many times formally affirmed the original immortality of the first man. Further, the Church formally decreed that God established the first man in holiness and justice. This picture is in sharp contrast with that given us by evolutionists, who depict the first humans as primitive creatures ascending by degrees from bestiality.

Genesis 2:8-14 gives a brief description of the Garden of Eden. The similar sounding Hebrew word "eden" means "delight." It is also called "Paradise", which is Greek for "Pleasure Park." The climate of the garden was mild, allowing "every tree that is pleasant to the sight and good for food" (2:9) to grow, and there were pleasant variations of temperature in the day (3:8). Adam and Eve had no need for clothing to protect them against the elements (2:25). A river flowed out of Eden to water the garden, and there it divided and became four rivers: the Pishon, the Gihon, the Tigris and the Euphrates. Though these latter two names are rivers existing today, there is no proof that they are the same rivers named in Genesis or located in the same area as the original rivers. Since the rivers in Eden flowed out of it, Eden must have been elevated. The description of Eden given in Genesis is probably Adam's own, as verses 11-14 are written in the present tense. There is no hint in Scripture or Tradition about the location of the Garden of Eden. Fossil evidence indicates that at one time the climate of the whole world was once temperate, and Genesis 1-11 makes no mention of cold, storms, hail, snow or lightning, nor any mention of falling rain before the Flood account.

In the garden God planted two special trees: the tree of life and the tree of knowledge of good and evil. There is no good reason to believe that these trees were not real. Both St. Augustine and St. Thomas Aquinas held that the tree of life was a cause of immortality because its fruit warded off bodily corruption that occurs with aging. The tree of the knowledge of good and evil had tempting fruit (3:6) that God used to test Adam's and Eve's obedience. Genesis need not be interpreted as saying that God made Adam first and then planted the garden afterward because that is the sequence in which they are mentioned. St. Augustine points out, "that the narrative, without mentioning it, refers to previous events that had been left unmentioned." The wording for the planting of the garden is such that it can be interpreted in either temporal sequence. But it makes more sense to say that it was planted before Adam was created and is mentioned after his creation because it was made for him. Concerning the two trees, besides having been real, they are types. The tree of life is a type of the Eucharist. As the tree of life nourished and preserved natural life, the Eucharist nourishes and preserves supernatural life. The tree of knowledge is a type of the Cross of Christ. The tree of knowledge tested Adam's obedience and he fell. The Cross tested Christ's obedience and He conquered.

Besides natural gifts like perfect bodies, an abundant variety of food and drink, and pleasant weather, God gave Adam and Eve certain other gifts. These were the gifts of freedom from suffering, infused knowledge, absence of concupiscence, and bodily immortality. They are called preternatural gifts because they are above and beyond the ordinary powers and capacities of human nature. They are also called gifts of integrity because they contribute to the uprightness and completeness of the human person. Finally, they are called relatively supernatural gifts because they are above the nature of man but not beyond created nature in general. For example, infused knowledge is natural for angels, but it is supernatural for human beings. The Pontifical Biblical Commission in 1909 upheld that Genesis affirms "the original happiness of our first parents in the state of justice, integrity, and immortality."

St Bonaventure made the point that the original bodies of Adam and Eve were without pain, even though they were able to suffer. He linked this with the innocence of their souls: "The body was so conformed to the soul that, as the soul was innocent and yet able to fall into sin, so the body was without pain and yet able to fall into suffering." Adam and Eve had complete peace of mind. There was no fear, no sadness, and perfect love and harmony between man and wife. There was also perfect harmony between the couple and the creatures about them. They were endowed with all the virtues. There was neither boredom nor weariness.

Since poisonous and thorny plants are a threat to the physical integrity of man, St. Augustine said they were created as a result of sin: "We should say, then, that the earth was cursed by reason of the sin of man so that it bears thorns; not that it should suffer punishment since it is without sensation but that it should always set before the eyes of man the judgment upon human sin. Thus men might be admonished by it to turn away from sins and turn to God's commandments. Poisonous plants were created as a punishment or as a trial for mortals. All this is the result of sin." But everything that God created is good in itself and created for a good reason. It seems that there were thorns and thistles and poisonous plants before the Fall because they were created for a purpose beneficial to man and posed no threat to our first parents. After the Fall, the thorns and the thistles interfered with Adam's farming (3:18). But that is not why God created them.

Adam enjoyed excellence in intelligence and knowledge. According to St. Cyril of Alexandria, "Our forefather Adam does not seem to have progressed gradually in wisdom as is the case with us, but immediately and from the very first days of his existence he is found perfected in intelligence, preserving in himself the enlightenment given him by God, still unsullied and pure, and having the dignity of his nature still unadulterated." And St. Thomas Aquinas spoke similarly: ". . . as the first man was produced in his perfect state, as regards his body, for the work of generation, so also was his soul established in a perfect state to instruct and govern others. Now no one can instruct others unless he has knowledge, and so the first man was established by God in such a manner as to have knowledge of all those things for which man has a natural aptitude."

Sacred Scripture suggests that there was perfect harmony in our first parents between reason and sensuality: "And the man and his wife were both naked, and were not ashamed" (2:25). God gifted them with free will and tempered all their emotions and appetites so as to be subject, at all times, to the dictates of reason. All the Fathers believed that Adam and Eve were free from concupiscence (irregular desire) in the garden; but they differed as to how this freedom was exercised. Some of the Fathers believed that Adam and Eve lived in the garden like sexless beings. For example, St John Chrysostom said that they "lived like angels, and there was no talk of cohabitation." St. Augustine, however, believed that there would have been sexual union if the Fall had not taken place, but it would have been free of lust. St. Thomas cites Augustine as saying that "our first parents did not come together in paradise, rather on account of sin were they ejected from paradise shortly after the creation of the woman; or because, having received the general Divine command relative to generation, they awaited the special command relative to time." Aquinas agrees with Augustine: "Therefore continence would not have been praiseworthy in the state of innocence, whereas it is praiseworthy in our present state, not because it removes fecundity, but because it excludes inordinate desire. In that state, fecundity would have been without lust."

St. Theophilus of Antioch said that God created man neither mortal nor immortal by nature. He made man capable of both, and man himself made the choice: "Someone, however, will say to us, 'Was man made by nature immortal?' Certainly not. 'Was he, then, immortal?' Neither do we say that. But someone will say, 'Was he, then, made nothing?' Not so, I reply. By nature, in fact, he was made neither mortal nor immortal. For if God had made him immortal from the very beginning, He would have made him God (-like). Again, if He had made him mortal, it would seem as if God were the cause of his death. He made him, then, neither mortal nor immortal, but, as we said above, capable of either. Thus if he should incline to the ways of immortality, keeping the commandment of God, he should receive from God the reward of immortality, and become God (-like). If, however, he turned aside to the ways of death, disobeying God, he should become for himself the cause of death. For God made man free and self-determining." St Augustine echoed that viewpoint, adding that the tree of life provided immortality.

It is impossible to conceive of a world before the Fall in which there were no dangers to man's life or limb. For example, fire still had the nature of fire, and man's body was material so it could be destroyed by fire. Physical immortality does not mean that our first parent's bodies were incapable of destruction, just as Mary's sinlessness does not mean that she was incapable of sin. It means that God preserved Adam and Eve from physical harm and bodily corruption just as He preserved Mary from sin. He preserved them from physical harm by divine providence and from bodily corruption through a special gift He gave to their souls. St. Thomas clearly explains that man was not incorruptible because his body had a disposition to incorruptibility, but because in his soul there was a power preserving the body from corruption: "For man's body was indissoluble not by reason of any intrinsic vigor of immortality, but by reason of a supernatural force given by God to the soul, whereby it was enabled to preserve the body from all corruption so long as it remained itself subject to God."

The supernatural, in an absolute sense, transcends the nature of creatures; no created nature has a claim to it. It is super-added to nature by God, and it presupposes a created nature because it exists in one. Therefore, the supernatural is not a substance but an accident; and it perfects the nature in which it operates because it affects the nature intrinsically by developing it to the divine order of being and activity. The greatest gift that God bestowed on our first parents was the supernatural gift of sanctifying grace, which is the gift of supernatural life that made them children of God and heirs to heaven. God created Adam and Eve in a state of innocence and holiness, which made them pleasing to God and full of love for Him. In Paradise, Adam and Eve enjoyed an intimacy with God greater than that of any prophet, including

Moses, and a supernatural destiny awaited them. Vatican Council I confirmed that God conferred a supernatural destiny on man: "God in His infinite goodness has ordained man for a supernatural end, namely, to participation in the divine goods which altogether surpass the understanding of the human mind, since 'eye hath not seen, nor ear heard, neither hath it entered into the heart of man, what things God hath prepared for them that love him' (1 Cor.2:9). The natural end of man is to know, love, and serve God with his natural powers. His supernatural end is to enjoy life with God in heaven. His nature, transformed by supernatural grace, is directed to that ultimate goal.

Man's life in Paradise, then, was a preparation for eternal life. Our first parents were able to merit supernatural reward, that is, greater enjoyment of God, by their acts. The Church teaches that such merit was not merely human and natural. The Catechism # 375 says, "The Church, interpreting the symbolism of biblical language in an authentic way, in the light of the New Testament and Tradition, teaches that our first parents, Adam and Eve, were constituted in an original 'state of holiness and justice.' This grace of original holiness was 'to share in . . . divine life.'" And # 376 continues, "By the radiance of this grace all dimensions of man's life were confirmed. As long as he remained in the divine intimacy, man would not have to suffer or die. (cf. Gn. 2:17; 3:16, 19). The inner harmony of the human person, the harmony between man and woman, (cf. Gn. 2:25) and finally, the harmony between the first couple and all creation, comprised the state called original justice."

It is obvious from its construction that God designed the human body for work. The capacity for and availability of work is a gift from God. Through his work, man cooperates with God in shaping creation and exercises his dominion over it. God provided work for the benefit of man; He did not create man for work. As the Catechism # 2428 says, "In work, the person exercises and fulfills in part the potential inscribed in his nature. The primordial value of labor stems from man himself, its author and its beneficiary. Work is for man, not man for work." St. Thomas Aquinas, like St. Augustine, says God gave man work in Paradise so that He might work in man, to sanctify man, and to give man pleasure. The Catechism # 378 points out that work in

Paradise is not a burden but collaboration with God: "The sign of man's familiarity with God is that God places him in the garden. (Gn. 2:8). There he lives 'to till and keep it.' Work is not yet a burden, (Gn. 2:15, 3:17-19) but rather the collaboration of man and woman with God in perfecting the visible creation." And the Catechism, #2427 & 2428, states that: "Human work proceeds directly from persons created in the image and likeness of God and called to prolong the work of creation by subduing the earth, both with and for one another. Hence work is a duty: 'If anyone will not work, let him not eat.' Work honors the Creator's gifts and the talents received from him . . . . Everyone should be able to draw from work the means of providing for his life and that of his family, and of serving the human community."

Isaiah prophesied: "I am God, there is no other; I am God, there is none like me. At the beginning I foretell the outcome; in advance, things not yet done. I say that my plan shall stand, I accomplish my every purpose." This verse shows that God has a master plan for creation that is being fulfilled in its history. The end is already there at the beginning because it is the reason for the beginning. The Old Testament prophets compare life in the Messianic era to the peaceful loving life in Paradise. For example, Hosea tells of the restoration of harmony between man and man and man and beast: "And I will make for you a covenant on that day with the beasts of the field, the birds of the air, and the creeping things of the ground; and I will abolish the bow, the sword, and war from the land; and I will make you lie down in safety." Revelation 20:1-3 tells us, "Then I saw an angel coming down from heaven, holding in his hand the key of the bottomless pit and a great chain. And he seized the dragon, that ancient serpent, who is the devil and Satan, and bound him for a thousand years, and threw him into the pit, and shut and sealed it over him, that he should deceive the nations no more, till the thousand years were ended. After that he must be loosed for a while." The Holy Office in 1944 decreed that Chiliasm, which states that Christ will rule visibly on earth before the final judgment, cannot be taught safely. But there is good reason to believe that there will be a great era of peace on earth before the end of time.

St. Gregory of Nyssa wrote that at the resurrection the bodies of the just will be changed into that which was at the beginning: "The resurrection promises us nothing else than the restoration of the fallen to their ancient state; for the grace we look for is a certain return to the first life, bringing back again to paradise those who were cast out from it. If then the life of those restored is closely related to that of the angels, it is clear that the life before the transgression was a kind of angelic life, and hence also our return to the ancient condition of life is compared to the angels." St. Augustine had a different view. He said that the flesh of the risen just will be restored to a better state than that of our first parents before they sinned. He goes so far as to say that their spiritualized bodies will have no need of physical nourishment. The bodies of the just "will be spiritual, not by ceasing to be bodies, but by being supported in their existence by a life-giving spirit . . . . The first man, however, was 'of the earth, earthly,' and he was made as a 'living soul,' not a 'life-giving spirit'; that condition was reserved for him after he merited it by obedience . . . . The body will thus be related to the life-giving spirit as it is now to the living soul."

St. Thomas summarizes the difference between the spirituality of our first parents and the spirituality of the elect: "In paradise man would have been like an angel in his spirituality of mind, yet with an animal life in his body. After the resurrection man will be like an angel, spiritualized in soul and body." He also says that Adam and Eve did not enjoy the Beatific Vision, as do the elect: "Man was happy in paradise, but not with that perfect happiness to which he was destined, which consists in the vision of the Divine Essence." Neither were they able to see the angels in their essence, as can the elect, because their souls' "connatural object (of knowledge) fell short of the excellence of separate substances."

Traditional Catholic theology holds that the risen bodies of the elect will have four properties that they do not now possess, according to the pattern of the risen body of Christ. First, impassibility; they will not be subject to death, corruption, pain, disease, hunger, thirst, fatigue or suffering of any kind. Second, agility; they will be able to move from place to place at the speed of thought. Third, subtility or spirituality; there will be no obstacle to their movement from place to place (recall how Christ appeared in the Upper Room with all the doors bolted). Fourth, radiance or brightness or clarity; the beauty of their souls will shine through their bodies with brilliance proportionate to their merits, (recall Christ's Transfiguration on Mt. Tabor).

The present world will be destroyed on the last day; Psalm 102 says, "They [heavenly bodies] will perish, but thou dost endure . . ." Isaiah echoes this in Is. 34:4 and in Is. 51:6; he says, "Lift up your eyes to the heavens, and look to the earth beneath; for the heavens will vanish like smoke, and the earth will wear out like a garment." St. Paul and St. John both foretell of the end of the present world; St Peter foretells the destruction of the world by fire, and Christ in Mt. 24:29 says, "But the day of the Lord will come like a thief, and then the heavens will pass away with a loud noise, and the elements will be dissolved with fire, and the earth and the works that are upon it will be burned up." The end of the world will be a supernatural event. Pope Pius II in 1459 condemned the notion that "the world should be naturally destroyed."

Scripture also says that the world will be restored on the last day; there will be a new heaven and a new earth. Isaiah and St. Peter both confirm this; while St. John describes in Rev. 21:1 his vision of a new heaven and a new earth: "Then I saw a new heaven and a new earth; for the first heaven and the first earth had passed away, and the sea was no more." In this new heaven and new earth there will be no need for the light of the sun or the moon (Rev. 22:5), "And night shall be no more; they need no light of lamp or sun, for the Lord God will be their light, and they shall reign forever and ever." This recalls the first day of Creation Week during which there was light without the sun. The Catechism # 1047 quoting St Irenaeus says, "The visible universe, then, is itself destined to be transformed, 'so that the world itself, restored to its original state, facing no further obstacles, should be at the service of the just,' sharing their glorification in the risen Jesus Christ." And in # 374 the Catechism says that the new creation in Christ will surpass the original in glory.

# DOCTRINE THIRTEEN

## The first man and woman sinned and lost the state of original happiness and innocence.

Genesis relates that God commanded Adam and Eve not to eat from the tree of the knowledge of good and evil. Eve, seduced by the devil in the form of a serpent, ate and enticed Adam to do so. In 1909 the Pontifical Biblical Commission, following the Fathers of the Church, ruled that "the divine command laid upon man to prove his obedience," and "the transgression of that divine command at the instigation of the devil under the form of a serpent," and "the fall of our first parents from their primitive state of innocence," and "the promise of a future Redeemer," are things in Genesis that must be taken in the "literal and historical sense" because they "pertain to the foundations of the Christian religion." As a consequence of their sin, Adam and Eve lost Paradise with many of its natural gifts, all the preternatural gifts and the gift of grace, for themselves and their progeny. The Council of Trent formally decreed that when Adam had transgressed the commandment of God in Paradise he immediately lost his holiness and the justice in which he had been established and that he was transformed in body and soul for the worse.

God commanded Adam not to eat from the tree of knowledge of good and evil (Gn. 2:17) to test his trust, faithfulness and obedience so that he might merit heaven. It was called the tree of the knowledge of good and evil, not because its fruit provided this knowledge, but because the test provided by the tree did. The Eastern Fathers tended to identify the tree with contemplative knowledge or self-knowledge. St. Gregory Nazianzen, without denying the literal reality of the tree of the knowledge of good and evil, said: "The tree was, according to my theory, contemplation, which is safe only for those who have reached maturity of habit to enter upon, but which is not good for those who are somewhat simple and greedy, just as neither is solid food good for those who are tender and have need of milk." St. John Chrysostom saw the tree of the knowledge of good and evil as being the object of contest, and the tree of life as being the reward for victory.

God accompanied His command with a threat, "you shall die," literally, "dying, you shall die." St. Augustine points out that the threat of death was threefold—spiritual, bodily and eternal: "His threat not only included the first part of the first death, that is, the soul's deprivation of God; not only the second part of the first death, the body's deprivation of the soul; not only the whole of the first death in which the soul, separated from both God and the body, is punished; but whatever of death is up to and including that absolutely final and so-called second death . . . in which the soul, deprived of God but united to the body, suffers eternal punishment." The Catechism # 396 gives a figurative interpretation for the tree of the knowledge of good and evil, but there is no good reason for denying its literal reality and the literal nature of God's command: "The 'tree of the knowledge of good and evil' (Gn. 2:17) symbolically invokes the insurmountable limits that man, being a creature, must freely recognize and respect with trust. Man is dependent on his Creator and subject to the laws of creation and to the moral norms that govern the use of freedom."

The temptation narrative begins with the appearance of Satan in the form of a serpent. Gen. 3:1 reads: "Now the serpent was more subtle than any other wild creature that the Lord God had made." There is a tendency among exegetes today to interpret this verse allegorically. However, St. Paul confirmed that the devil actually took the form of a serpent: "But I am afraid that as the serpent deceived Eve by his cunning, your thoughts will be led astray from a sincere and pure devotion to Christ" (2 Cor. 11:3). And the interpretation of the Fathers was quite realistic. Following them, the Pontifical Biblical Commission in 1909 stated that the temptation of Eve by the devil "under the guise of a serpent" is one of the things in Genesis that must be taken in the "literal and historical sense" because it "pertains to the foundations of the Christian religion." Any figurative or symbolic meaning in the devil taking the form of a serpent must be understood in that light. For example, Pope John Paul II referred to Satan as "symbolized by the serpent." This does not mean that the serpent was not real; it means that Satan took the form of a serpent to represent himself as one would costume himself to project an identity, as in St Luke's Gospel, Chapter 8 wherein demons entered into the swine. St. Ephrem said that the serpent was more cunning than the other animals yet he was not a rational animal but, "As for the serpent's speech, either Adam understood the serpent's own mode of communication, or Satan spoke through it, or the serpent posed the question in his mind and speech was given to it. Or Satan sought from God that speech be given to the serpent for a short time." St. John Damascene writes similarly but personalizes the serpent as being on intimate terms with man and conversing agreeably with him. St. Cyprian of Carthage gives us the motive for Satan's scheming: "The devil bore impatiently the fact that man was made in the image of God; and that is why he (the devil) was first to perish and the first to bring others to perdition."

The serpent said to Eve (Gn. 3:1): "Did God say, 'You shall not eat of any tree of the garden?' "This is Satan's subtle entry. He probably said it with an incredulous tone of voice with the *implication*, "How could He do that?", thereby slyly opening the forum at once to questioning God's word. No doubt, he knew that it was only the tree of the knowledge of good and evil that was forbidden. But he couldn't come right out and question that. That would be a frontal attack on God's authority. Rather he questioned something that seemed unreasonable, which both he and Eve knew wasn't true. The deadly conversation continues: "And the woman said to the serpent, 'We may eat of the fruit of the trees of the garden; but God said 'You shall not eat of the fruit of the tree which is in the midst of the garden, neither shall you touch it, lest you die.' But the serpent said to the woman, 'You will not die. For God knows then when you eat of it your eyes will be opened, and you will be like God, knowing good and evil.'" The serpent lied when he said they will not die; but he was telling the truth when he said they would become like God, knowing good and evil (Gn. 3:5). That's how the devil works, admixing truth with lies. The truth is the bait, the lie is the hook.

St. Ambrose said that Satan approached Eve rather than Adam because she did not receive the command directly from God and was therefore an easier target, so Satan ". . . aimed to circumvent Adam by means of the woman. He did not accost the man who had in his presence received the heavenly command." St. Bonaventure tells us that Satan's temptation was threefold: "The devil enticed woman through a triple desire, namely, by knowledge which corresponds to the rational desire, by excellence in the mode of God which corresponds to the irascible desire, and by the sweetness of the tree which corresponds to the concupiscent desire. Thus he lured all that was temptable in woman and through which she could be led to temptation, and this is the triple desire of the world, namely, 'the concupiscence of the flesh and the concupiscence of the eyes, and the pride of life' (1 John 2:16). The origin of all temptation lies in these three: the world, the flesh, and the devil."

St. Ephrem sees in Eve's eating first, the desire to dominate her husband: "She hastened to eat before her husband that she might become head over her head, that she might be the one to give command to that one by whom she was to be commanded and that she might be older in divinity than that one who was older than she in humanity." The sin was a sin of disobedience to God by the literal eating of the forbidden fruit. The root of the disobedience was pride: 'you will be like God" (Gn. 3:5). The eating of the fruit is not symbolic of sexual sin as ancient and modern commentators have proposed. Those who look for symbolic meanings in opposition to the literal meaning do injustice to the text. One wonders why they do not accept the narrative as it stands because it gives a credible and consistent account of the first sin. The Catechism (# 397-398) summarizes the story of man's first sin: "Man, tempted by the devil, let his trust in his Creator die in his heart and, abusing his freedom, disobeyed God's command. This is what man's first sin consisted of . . . In that sin, man preferred himself to God and by that very act scorned Him. He chose himself over and against God, against the requirements of his creaturely status and thereafter against his own good. Constituted in a state of holiness, man was destined to be fully 'divinized' by God in glory. Seduced by the devil, he wanted to 'be like God' but 'without God, before God, and not in accordance with God'" (St. Maximus the Confessor). Eve first sinned against the virtue of Faith by doubting God's truthfulness and love. She doubted His truthfulness when she allowed herself to be led into disbelieving God's warning, "you shall die," and she doubted His love when she became suspicious about God's motive for forbidding them to eat from the tree of knowledge. Genesis does not say explicitly that she committed those sins, but it implies so.

If Adam and Eve had been faithful to God, they would have passed, without suffering or dying, from Paradise to heaven, where they would see God face to face. Because of their sin, Adam and Eve lost sanctifying grace and the preternatural gifts. Having lost sanctifying grace, they lost the friendship of God and the right to heaven. God drove them out of Paradise and barred their reentry (Gn. 3:23-24), removing from them access to the tree of life. They became subject to suffering, toil and death (Gn. 3:16-19); their minds and wills were weakened; and they acquired an inclination to evil. St. Augustine expressed the consequences in terms of decay and chaos: "The effect of that sin was to subject human nature to all the process of decay which we see and feel, and consequently to death also. And man was distracted and tossed about by violent and conflicting emotions, a very different being from what he was in paradise before his sin, though even then he lived in an animal body."

In its decree on original sin the Council of Trent said: "If anyone does not confess that the first man Adam, when he transgressed the commandment of God in Paradise, immediately lost his holiness and the justice in which he had been established, and that he incurred through the offense of that prevarication the wrath and indignation of God and hence the death with which God had previously threatened him—and with death's captives under his power, who thenceforth 'had the empire of death' (Heb. 2:14), that is of the devil—and through that offense of prevarication the entire Adam was transformed in body and soul for the worse, let him be anathema." The immediate consequence of the sin of Adam and Eve, which they suffered even before encountering God, was awareness of their nakedness (Gn. 3:7). Earlier the sacred author (Gn. 2:25) pointed out that they were both naked and not ashamed. Now they are ashamed of their nakedness, and they fashion fig leaves to cover themselves. Later God will clothe them with garments of skins (Gn. 3:21). Following their sin, "the eyes of both were opened" to a new law operating in them, which St. Paul described: "I see in my members another law at war with the law of my mind and making me captive to the law of sin which dwells in my members." St. Ephrem said that Adam and Eve were ashamed because their bodies lost their cloaks of glory: "They were not ashamed (before the Fall) because of the glory with which they were clothed. It was when this glory was stripped from them after they had transgressed the commandment that they were ashamed because they were naked."

After they covered themselves, Adam and Eve heard God walking in the garden. This need not be taken as an anthropomorphism. God took on a human appearance before the Incarnation when he appeared to Abraham by the oaks of Mamre. So it is not hard to believe that he conversed with Adam in human form as they walked together through the garden. St. Ephrem says that God allowed His footsteps to be heard so they could prepare to make supplication before Him. They were so frightened they tried to hide from God. God called out to Adam, asking where he was, and Adam replied that he was frightened by God's footsteps because he was naked. God asked Adam how he knew he was naked and then asked if he had eaten of the forbidden fruit. The question, of course, was a reproof since God knew what had happened. These events marked the end of the perfect harmony between man and woman. Adam blamed Eve and she in turn blamed the serpent and neither took responsibility for their sin. St. Ephrem said, "If Adam and Eve had sought to repent after they had transgressed the commandment, even though they would not have regained that which they possessed before their transgression of the commandment, they would have escaped from the curses that were decreed on the earth and upon them." God cursed the serpent first. His wrath was directed not at the animal but at the evil spirit that resided in it, however, his curse applied to both. The evil spirit will suffer spiritually what the animal has to suffer physically. Although the serpent, as an animal, was free of guilt, it was cursed on account of Adam's sin, as was all nature. But it was cursed "above all cattle and above all wild animals" (Gn. 3:14) as a sign of the curse on Satan.

Genesis 3:15 is called the Protoevangelium (First Gospel) because it is the first announcement of the good news of the Redeemer. It wasn't presented as a promise to Adam and Eve but as a curse on the devil. He was being told that his days were numbered. The devil and his followers will be put at enmity with the woman, whom the Church has always seen as the mother of the Savior, and her seed, her Son the Messiah and Savior of the world. He is the new Adam who, because he became obedient unto death, even death upon a cross, atoned for the disobedience of Adam. Satan will strike at the heel of His Mystical Body, the Catholic Church, and bruise it. But He will crush the head of the serpent through the instrumentality of His mother. Mary is the new Eve. Like Eve she was created without sin, but unlike Eve she never sinned. The first Eve was the first to succumb to the influence of the devil. Mary, the new Eve, will destroy his influence forever.

Through a woman Satan entered the world, and through a woman he will take leave of it. St. John had a vision of his destruction: "And the devil who had deceived them was thrown into the lake of fire and brimstone where the beast and the false prophet were, and they will be tormented day and night forever and ever" (Rev. 20:10). The Lord would punish Adam and Eve for their sin, but He would not abandon them. God started to unfold His plan for sending a Savior to reopen the gates of heaven. But why did He allow our first parents to sin to begin with? The Catechism (# 412) explains that He allowed this to bring about an infinitely great good, the Incarnation, citing St. Leo the Great who said, "Christ's inexpressible grace gave us blessings better than those the demon's envy had taken away;" and St. Thomas Aquinas wrote, "There is nothing to prevent human nature's being raised up to something greater, even after sin; God permits evil in order to draw forth some greater good. Thus St. Paul says, 'Where sin increased, grace abounded all the more.'"

St. Ephrem said that God punished the serpent first to instill fear in Adam and Eve so that they might repent; and when they didn't, God proceeded to punish them. God punished Eve first because it was through her that sin was passed on to Adam. She was first cursed to bear suffering in childbirth. Natural processes of the body produce pleasurable sensations (when operating properly). So would childbirth have done if there were no Fall. The second punishment Eve suffered was subjection to Adam. According to St. John Chrysostom, this was not part of God's original plan. Although there was equality of status before the Fall, Chrysostom makes it clear that Adam was the head of the human race and therefore had a responsibility for guiding and correcting Eve: "After all, you are head of your wife, and she has been created for your sake; but you have inverted the proper order: not only have you failed to keep her on the straight and narrow but you have been dragged down with her, and whereas the rest of the body should follow the head, the contrary has in fact occurred, the head following the rest of the body, turning things upside down."

Eve's punishment was connected with her mission to be the womb of the human species. Adam's punishment was connected with the mission God gave him to till the soil and make it fruitful (Gen. 2:15, 3:17, 23). Before his sin Adam always experienced pleasurable sensations when exercising the various faculties God gave him. There was no admixture of drudgery with pleasure as there is in work today. And the earth cooperated perfectly with his efforts. The thorns and thistles that were later to become scourges to him then worked to his benefit. After his sin things would be different. There would be much toil against a resistant earth in making it fruitful so that he and Eve and their children may eat.

God then tells Adam that in the end his body will become one with the earth because he will die. Theodore of Cyr said that the death sentence was a mixture of love with punishment. It "brings evil works to an end" and "ends the suffering of the body." St. Ambrose said that Adam himself, and not God, was the agent of his own death: "Still another problem arises. 'From what source did death come to Adam? Was it from the nature of a tree of this sort or actually from God?' . . . The solution, unless I am mistaken, lies in the fact that since disobedience was the cause of death, for that very reason not God but man himself was the agent of his own death."

God said to Adam: "Cursed is the ground because of you" (Gen. 3:17). All creation suffers corruptibility as the effect of Adam's sin. St. Paul referred to this in his epistle to the Romans. He said that creation was "subjected to futility," has been "groaning in travail," and is in "bondage to decay." The phrase "bondage to decay" does not imply that there was no decomposition of matter before the Fall. It is the nature of matter to change. Decomposition is the breaking down of ordered matter into its constituent parts. It serves a useful purpose if the constituent parts are recomposed into other ordered material structures, as happens with living organisms. The result is that order is maintained. The process of recomposition requires the intervention of an intelligent agent, as in the case of the Designer of living organisms. Decomposition before the Fall was useful and served man. Decay or corruption is useless decomposition; the constituent parts do not enter into new ordered structures, thus order is lost. After the Fall, the process of decay causes a continual loss of order in the universe, which often counters man's welfare. This is called the law of morpholysis (loosening of structure.) It has been formulated mathematically in the second law of thermodynamics.

With its renewal at the end of time, the world will be restored to a state of incorruptibility. It "will be set free from its bondage to decay" (Rom. 8:21). But first it will be destroyed to complete the process of decomposition. St. Cyril of Alexandria, commenting on Romans 8:19-23, connects the transformation of creation at the end of time with the glorification of the just: "But by the secret plan of God, which orders all things for the best, it will come to this end. For when the sons of God, who have lived a righteous life, have been transformed into glory from dishonor and from what is corruptible into what is incorruptible, then will creation too be transformed into something better." (See Rom. 8:21; Cor. 15:54).

# DOCTRINE FOURTEEN

# The whole human species descended from the first man and woman.

Genesis makes it explicitly clear that Adam and Eve were the first human beings from whom the whole human species descended. Pope Pius II in 1459 excluded the existence of pre-Adamites and colonization from outer space by condemning the notions that Adam was not the first man and that God created another world. Pope Pius XII in 1950 explicitly rejected polygenism. The Church formally teaches that God specially creates each human soul at conception, that every descendant of Adam and Eve, with the exception of Jesus and Mary, is conceived with original sin, and that original sin is transmitted by propagation and not by imitation.

Sacred Scripture explicitly testifies that Adam and Eve were the first human beings from whom the whole human species descended: "And there was no man to till the ground" (Gen. 2:5). "The man called his wife's name Eve because she was the mother of all the living" (Gen. 3:20). "And he made from one every nation of men to live on all the face of the earth" (Acts 17:26). Thus there were no "pre-Adamites" and no primordial community of more than two. St. Ambrose said that the flesh of man and woman is of one nature and that there is only one source for the human race. St. Augustine said: "In that very beginning Adam and Eve were the parents of all peoples . . . ."

Theodoret of Cyr said that "the myriads of tribes came from one couple," so that men might not suppose that there was any difference in their natures. One might say that Theodoret was a fifth-century anti-racist anticipating future Enlightenment intellectuals and Darwinists who would classify the different races (tribes) as different species and therefore different in nature. Also, the human species is not a "race." A race is a variety within a species; all races within a species have the same nature. The term "human race" is not a proper term because it implies that there are nonhuman races that have the same nature as humans. Writing in the 1950s, Cardinal Ernesto Ruffini emphasized the importance of the doctrine of the unity of the human species: "It is a truth of Faith that the human species is one, and that all men spring from the same two parents. It could be said that this is one of the most fundamental truths of the Catholic religion. We shall go further: to impugn this basic principle would be to attack the very existence of Christianity." As the cardinal indicated, the Church has spoken on the unity of the human race. It is important to her because it is a prerequisite for the dogmas concerning original sin and redemption. Pope Pius II in 1459 excluded the existence of pre-Adamites and colonization from outer space by condemning the proposition: "That God created another world than this one, and that, in its time, many other men and women existed and that, consequently, Adam was not the first man." The Pontifical Commission in 1909 decreed that "the oneness of the human race" is a fact that "pertain(s) to the foundation of the Catholic religion."

In "Humani generis" Pope Pius XII definitely ruled out polygenism, which was inferred from an evolutionary interpretation of human fossils: "When there is a question of another conjectural opinion, of polygenism so-called, then the sons of the Church in no way enjoy such freedom (of inquiry). For the faithful in Christ cannot accept this view, which holds that either after Adam there existed men on this earth, who did not receive their origin by natural generation from him, the first parent of all; or that Adam signifies some kind of multitude of first parents; for it is by no means apparent how such an opinion can be reconciled with what the sources of revealed truth and the acts of the Magisterium of the Church teaches about original sin, which proceeds from a sin truly committed by Adam, and which is transmitted to all by generation, and exists in each one as his own." Pius XII closed discussion on the question of polygenism; and Pope Paul VI affirmed this saying: "It is evident that you will not consider as reconcilable with authentic Catholic doctrine those explanations of original sin, given by some authors, which start from the presupposition of polygenism which is not proved . . . ." Pius XII didn't ask theologians to study whether polygenism is reconcilable with Catholic dogma; he told them that it is not. This is again reaffirmed in the Catechism # 360.

The human soul is not propagated by natural generation like the human body. Rather God infuses each human soul in a special act of creation. Eve implied this when she said: "I have gotten a man with the help of the Lord" (Gen. 4:1). Several other Scripture passages allude to the special creation of the soul (Ez. 21:30, 28:13, 15, Eccl.12: 7, Wis. 15:11). St. Jerome says, "Whence did Cain and Abel, the first offspring of the first human beings, have their souls? And the whole human race afterward, what do you suppose is the origin of their souls? Was it from propagation like the brute animals, in such a way that just as body comes from body so too is soul generated from soul? . . . God is engaged daily in making souls; God for whom to will is to have done and who never ceases to be the Creator." St. Augustine castigated the notion that the human soul is generated through the semen, saying that the soul would then be corporeal, but left open the question of soul being generated by soul. Pope Pius XII in "Humani generis" taught that the "Catholic Faith obliges us to hold that souls are immediately created by God." The Catechism # 366 summarizes the Church's teaching on the origin and destiny of the human soul: "The Church teaches that every spiritual soul is created immediately by God—it is not 'produced' by the parents—and also that it is immortal: it does not perish when it separates from the body at death, and it will be reunited with the body at the final Resurrection." Created "immediately" means created at the moment of conception. "From the time that the ovum is fertilized, a life is begun which is neither that of the father nor of the mother; it is rather the life of a new human being with his own growth. It would never be made human if it were not human already" (Declaration on Procured Abortion CDF Nov. 18, 1974).

Adam at the suggestion of the devil sinned, and as a consequence of his sin Adam was changed for the worse in body and soul and fell under the power of the devil. Furthermore, his damaged nature was passed on to his whole progeny, who, like him suffer mortality, pain, weakened intellects and wills, an inclination to evil from which they cannot completely free themselves, and subjection to the power of the devil. Sin and death enter together with the murder of Abel by Cain (Gen. 4:8). Sin spread for some 1600 years until the earth was filled with corruption and violence (Gen. 6:11-12), to the point where God decided to destroy the earth and its inhabitants and start anew with eight survivors, Noah, his wife, their three sons and their wives. Adam's sin caused him to pass on a damaged nature to his posterity, but not a completely corrupted nature. His descendants, even though their wills were weakened, still retained the freedom to resist their inclination to evil; and even though their intellects were darkened, they still could come to know of the existence of God with their natural power of cognition. Scripture attests to this (Gen.4:7, Rom. 1:20).

David the Psalmist sang mournfully: "Behold I was brought forth in iniquity and in sin did my mother conceive me" (Ps. 51:5). And Rom. 5:18-19 tells us ". . . one man's trespass led to condemnation for all men . . . by one man's disobedience all were made sinners . . ." Thus all of Adam's descendants, with the exception of the Blessed Virgin Mary and her Son, are conceived without the gift of supernatural life, that is, sanctifying grace. They are born without the friendship of God and the right to heaven. This state of deprivation is called original sin. St. Augustine stated: "In Adam all sinned when, by that power innate in his nature, by which he was able to beget them, all were as yet the one Adam." Augustine further said that we imitate Adam when we sin, but original sin is transmitted not by imitation but by propagation: "Adam, in whom all die, besides being an example for imitation to those who willfully transgress the commandment of the Lord, by the hidden depravity of his own carnal concupiscence, depraved in his own person all those who came from his stock . . . 'Through one man,' the Apostle says, 'sin entered the world, through sin death' (Rom. 5:12). And this refers not to imitation but propagation."

The contraction of original sin is connected with the nature not the person. It is called "sin" only in an analogical sense: it is sin contracted and not committed—a state not an act. The Church has always insisted that it is passed on by natural generation, by propagation, and not by imitation, as the Catechism # 404 says. Also we read there, "How did the sin of Adam become the sin of all his descendants? The whole human race is in Adam 'as one body of one man' (St. Thomas Aquinas, De Malo 4, 1). By this 'unity of the human race' all men are implicated in Adam's sin, as all are implicated in Christ's justice. Still, the transmission of original sin is a mystery that we cannot fully understand. But we do know by Revelation that Adam had received original holiness and justice not for himself alone, but for all human nature." Genesis itself does not give explicit doctrine on original sin, or explicitly whether Adam and Eve were reconciled with God, though this is implied. However the Book of Wisdom (Wis. 10:1) affirms that Adam was delivered from his transgression: "Wisdom protected the first-formed father of the world, when he alone had been created; she delivered him from his transgression, and gave hum strength to rule all things."

The world from the creation of Adam and Eve to the Great Flood was a very different world from ours. It was in the beginning, and the laws of development were different, too, just as the laws for the development of an embryo differ from those of an adult. St Augustine said, "These first works of God are, of course, unparalleled just because they are first. Those who refuse to believe in them ought to refuse credence to any unusual phenomena. But in fact these events would not be classed as extraordinary, if they had occurred in the normal course of nature. For no event is without purpose under the all-embracing government of God's providence, even if the reason for it is hidden from us."

Before proceeding, here are a few words about biblical chronology. Biblical chronology is a reliable guide for determining the approximate age of the human species, which is that of the earth, despite the variations in the text and the possibility of omissions in the genealogies. F. N. Jones in 1999 compiled a list of the dates of Creation as calculated by 30 different scholars. They range from 3836 B.C. to 5426 B.C., the most famous being 4004 B.C., calculated by James Ussher.

St. Augustine reckoned "from the evidence of Holy Scripture that fewer than 6000 years have passed since man's first origin." He argues from historical records available to him to refute "the nonsense of the writings which allege many more thousands of years, and to show how utterly inadequate is their authority on this subject." He could write the same thing today. In his day he had to refute false history. Today he would have to refute false science. Evolutionary anthropologists "controvert the authority of our sacred books" by telling us the human species is hundreds of thousands or even millions of years old. But they can't make up their minds exactly how old. This is a reflection of the total unreliability of the dating methods they use, as was discussed before. Suffice it to say here that we need not worry about being contradicted by the facts of science, as opposed to the speculations of scientists, if we accept the biblical testimony that the human species has been around only a few thousand years.

At the outset there was marriage between brothers and sisters in order that the human species might grow. This is one of the original laws of development that is no longer applicable. The first descendant of Adam and Eve mentioned in Scripture is Cain. But that does not necessarily mean he was their first offspring. It only means he was the first child of significance in the history of salvation, as Genesis 4:14 speaks of the earth already being populated when God exiled him after he murdered Abel. Genesis gives us some information of the various descendants of Adam and Eve, which we will not go into here. Suffice it to say that antediluvian people lived longer lives than we do today. Man had lost the gift of immortality but still had the gift of a long life; only after Noah's flood did the human life span decrease to its present length. The antediluvian patriarchs found in Genesis lived spans ranging from 365 years to 969 years. Many today scoff at these long life spans given in Scripture but accept without question billions of years for the age of the earth, even if those estimates vary by hundreds of millions of years. So why should we not accept the biblical record in this regard?

Besides being long-lived, there is evidence of antediluvians of great stature. Genesis 6:4 says, "The Nephilim were on the earth in those days." The Nephilim was a race of giants. St. Augustine said that we know from Scripture and from Hebrew and Christian traditions that in the period before the Flood there were many giants, though not all the antediluvians were giants. He also offers historical evidence for giants living after the flood. There is also fossil evidence for the existence of giants in the past. R. L. Wysong provides photos of such evidence along with documentary information. In his book "The Creation-Evolution Controversy" (1976) he writes, "Human footprints, both normal size and giant size, sometimes side by side with dinosaur prints, have been found in Mexico, New Mexico, Arizona, Texas, Missouri, Kentucky, Illinois and other U.S. locations." The earth on which the antediluvians lived was much different from what it is today. That world was destroyed by the Great Flood. By the time of the Flood the human species had been in existence more than 1600 years, had probably spread throughout the whole earth, and spoke the same language or dialects thereof.

Since much of the water that is now on the surface of the earth was either beneath it or above it (some theorize a form of vapor canopy), there would have been a larger landmass to support the superabundance of life. The geography and topography was different and probably gentler, as the Great Flood greatly reshaped the earth's surface producing the rugged topography we have today. The fossil record shows that there was once a great abundance and rich variety of plant and animal life, which the Flood transformed into huge deposits of coal and oil. The water vapor canopy theory envisions, among other things, a uniform and moderate climate. Some speculate that this climate could also have come from a network of warm ocean currents. Many of these gifts of the pre-Flood world were lost in the Flood's aftermath. Whenever God punishes people for sin by withdrawing gifts from them, their posterity also suffer this loss; but God is good and merciful and often replaces such lost gifts with others, even better ones.

# DOCTRINE FIFTEEN

## God destroyed the world that was with a worldwide flood.

S cripture and Tradition clearly proclaim the historical fact that a worldwide flood destroyed the earth in the time of Noah. The Flood blotted out all men and all land-living animals except those on the ark. Signs of the Flood abound in the legends of all peoples and in the geological features of the earth.

Genesis 6:5-8 tells us that as the antediluvian world grew, sin increased. The people became so hardened in sin that God saw fit to destroy the whole world along with all the people in it, except for one righteous man named Noah, his wife, and his three sons and their wives. This text attributes human emotion to God. He is said to be sorry and grieved. It seems as if He is angry and has second thoughts. St. Augustine points out that Scripture attributes human emotions to God for the sake of man: "Now God's anger is not an agitation of his mind; it is a judgment by which punishment is inflicted on sin. And his consideration and reconsideration are his unchanging plan applied to things subject to change. For God does not repent of any action of his, (cf. Num. 23:19) as man does, and his decision on any matter whatsoever is as fixed as his foreknowledge is sure. But if Scripture did not employ such words, it would not strike home so closely, as it were, to all mankind." He goes on to explain that the text speaks of the destruction of animals not because they were guilty of sin but to project the magnitude of the coming disaster.

The Fathers of the Church taught that God had given the antediluvians 120 years to repent, but they refused to do so. That is how the Fathers interpreted Genesis 6:3 which states: "Then the Lord said: 'My spirit shall not abide in man forever, for he is flesh, but his days shall be 120 years.'" St. Ephrem says that if they had repented they could have saved themselves from the Flood: "This generation will not live nine hundred years like the previous generations, for it is flesh and its days are filled with the deeds of flesh. Therefore, their days will be one hundred and twenty years. If they repent during this time, they will be saved from the wrath that is about to come upon them." St. Jerome asserted that the 120 years referred to a period of repentance and not the lifespan of man. He also said that because of man's utter recalcitrance, God reduced that period to 100 years: "Since they indeed despised to do repentance, God was unwilling for his decree to await its time, but, cutting off the space of twenty years, He brought on the flood in the one hundredth year that had been destined for doing repentance."

Noah pleased God. "Noah was a righteous man, blameless in his generation; Noah walked with God" (Gen. 6:9).Since his generation was totally corrupt, Noah's virtue shined even more brightly. According to St. John Chrysostom, "Virtue in fact is admirable even for itself. If someone cultivates virtue among those who refuse it, he makes it more worthy of admiration. Therefore the Scriptures, as though in admiration of this just man, point out the contrast: that only one man who was living among those who soon would experience the wrath of God, this Noah, 'found favor in the eyes of the Lord God.'" Scripture singled out Noah for special praise because he was blameless "at that time when the obstacles to virtue were many." Apparently Noah and his family were the only just people on earth at the time of the Flood. The account does not say that Noah preached to the antediluvians, though Christian tradition holds this to be so, as St. Peter (2 Peter 2:5) called Noah a "preacher of holiness."

God told Noah to build an ark in which he and his family were to be rescued from the flood of waters God was going to send upon the earth. God gave Noah detailed instructions about the construction of the ark: "Make yourself an ark of gopher wood; make rooms in the ark, and cover it inside and out with pitch. This is how you are to make it; the length of the ark three hundred cubits, its breadth fifty cubits, and its height thirty cubits. Make a roof for the ark, and finish it to a cubit above; and set the door of the ark in its side; make it with lower, second, and third decks" (Gen. 6:14-16). The Fathers reckoned that God gave Noah a hundred years to build the ark, probably because Scripture says that Noah's sons were born after he was five hundred years old, and the Flood began when he was six hundred years old (Gen. 5:32 & 7:6). God gave Noah certain instructions on loading the ark: "But I will establish my covenant with you; and you shall come into the ark, you, your sons, your wife, and your sons' wives with you. And every living thing of all flesh, you shall bring two of every sort into the ark, to keep them alive with you; they shall be male and female. Of the birds according to their kinds, of every creeping thing of the ground according to its kind, two of every sort shall come to you to keep them alive. Also take with you every sort of food that is eaten, and store it up; it shall serve as food for you and for them" (Gen.6:18-21). He also told Noah to take additional clean animals and birds, seven pairs of each; some of those will be used for sacrifice after the Flood (Gen. 7:2-3, 9:20).

There was supernatural assistance in the collection of animals. The text makes it clear that God sent the animals to Noah; he did not have to collect them. God informed their instincts at the appropriate times to migrate towards the ark. There were no barriers to their migration in the antediluvian world as there are in the postdiluvian world. There may have been only one landmass, or if there were more than one landmass there was probably a complete collection of animals on each, at least on the one where Noah lived. And all the animals need not have been full grown. Of the very large animals, very young ones may have been taken aboard to minimize space and feeding problems. Many animals may have entered into either natural or supernaturally induced hibernation, thereby minimizing feeding and waste disposal problems. St. Ephrem said that God "established a state of peace between the predatory animals and those who are preyed upon." Noah took on only creatures that needed to be put on the ark for survival. Creatures that did not need to be put on the ark to survive, for example, fish, were left to fend for themselves during the Flood.

St. Augustine insisted the biblical account of the Flood is both historical and allegorical: ". . . no one, however stubborn, will venture to imagine that this narrative was written without an ulterior purpose; and it could not plausibly be said that the events, though historical, have no symbolic meaning, or that the account is not factual, but merely symbolical, or that the symbolism has nothing to do with the Church. No, we must believe that the writing of this historical record had a wise purpose, that the events are historical, that they have a symbolic meaning, and that this meaning gives a prophetic picture of the Church." Augustine saw Noah's ark as a symbol of the Church on pilgrimage in the world. It is a haven made safe by the wood of the ark, which represents the wood of the Cross on which Christ saved us. The Catechism # 845, recalls an "image dear to the Church Fathers, she (the Church) is prefigured by Noah's ark, which alone saves from the flood." It also recalls 1 Peter 3:21 saying, ". . . the flood and Noah's ark prefigured salvation by Baptism."

God directed Noah to take the animals and his family on to the ark. Noah did as God commanded. The loading took seven days. The animals entered the ark two-by-two, and when all the occupants were aboard God closed the ark and then the rain came (Gen. 7:1-16). The Flood was a supernaturally induced unleashing of natural powers, for God said he would send the rain upon the earth. He collapsed the antediluvian vapor blanket (if there was one), released pressurized subterranean waters, and perhaps induced volcanic activity as well. The Flood was worldwide because it covered all the mountains by at least thirty feet and killed all living creatures that lived on land (Gen. 7:19-23). Noah, his wife, his three sons and their wives were the only human beings that survived the Flood. Christ himself confirmed this: "They ate, they drank, they married, they were given in marriage, until the day when Noah entered the ark, and the flood came and destroyed them all" (Lk. 17:27).

It would be naïve to suppose that the Flood was a tranquil affair, like the filling and the draining of a bathtub. Every one knows that small local floods lasting only hours produce great changes in landscape. So it should not be hard to believe that a furious flood of rain over the whole earth for forty days and forty nights could completely reshape the face of the earth. The Flood piled layer upon layer of sediment to form the mountains. Plants and animals were buried rapidly in the sediments to form fossils. Massive collections of plant and animal debris were compressed under great pressures to form oil and coal deposits. Great tectonic movements caused by the weight of the water sitting for one hundred and fifty days, and apparently aided by divine intervention, caused the continents to rise and the sea floors to sink. Thus "the waters of the earth receded from the earth continually." This process lasted for another one hundred and fifty days (Gen. 7:24, 8:1-3).

The Flood obviously was not a local one, as some maintain, because if that were the case God could just have told Noah to move to another area rather than go to the trouble of building a gigantic ark. And a local flood would not have killed all the inhabitants of the earth. Further, God's promise in Genesis 9:11 that the earth would never again be destroyed by a flood would be meaningless if He was speaking of a local flood. Local floods do not destroy the earth, although they do great damage on it. And if it weren't a meaningless promise, it would have been a broken promise because there have been innumerable, local floods since the Genesis Flood.

Exactly five months after the rain began the ark came to rest on the mountains of Ararat. Two months and thirteen days later the tops of the mountains could be seen (Gen. 8:4-5). These were probably new mountains being raised as the waters drained into permanent basins. The original antediluvian mountains were probably eroded away by the Flood. The waters were dried off from the earth ten months and thirteen days after the rains began (Gen. 7:11, 8:13). Forty days after observing the mountain tops, Noah sent out a raven that "went to and fro until the waters were dried up from the earth" (Gen. 8:6-7). Later Noah sent out a dove, but it returned to the ark because it found no place to set foot because the earth was still covered with water. Seven days later he sent it out again and it returned with an olive branch, indicating that the waters had subsided. Seven days after that Noah sent the dove out again but it did not return, indicating that the earth was ready to be occupied (Gen. 8:8-11).

God directed Noah to leave the ark along with his family and the animals. Noah then built an altar to the Lord and offered burnt offerings of every clean animal. God was pleased with the offering and in turn promised never to curse the ground again because of man's transgressions, never to destroy every living creature again by water, and to maintain the regularity of the seasons, which had been disturbed during the Flood (Gen 8:20-22, 9:15).

The Genesis account is the only completely true and authoritative account of the Great Flood. It is a sober, detailed and consistent report that was written by eyewitnesses. The post-diluvian patriarchs preserved it faithfully and passed it on to their posterity intact. Eventually it reached Moses, through whom the divine seal was put on it, certifying its accuracy. Other peoples, not in the line of the patriarchs, drifted away from the true religion. They recalled the story of the Deluge, but because of their lack of devotion to the one true God, they corrupted it, transforming it into fantastic tales. Such tales are found in the traditions of nearly all peoples throughout the world—in those of the most advanced civilizations and the most barbarous tribes. Although they may differ in details, the tales generally agree that there was a destruction of all human beings by water and that an ark or boat provided the means for some to survive and repopulate the world. Many also attribute the Flood to the wickedness of man.

The first century Jewish historian Flavius Josephus records that there were stories about the Flood and the ark in Gentile nations and that there were even reports that there were remains of the ark: "Now all the writers of barbarian histories make mention of the flood and this ark; among whom is Berosus the Chaldean; for when he is describing the circumstances of the flood, he goes on thus: 'It is said that there is still some part of this ship in Armenia, at the mountain of the Cordyaeans; and that some people carry off pieces of the bitumen, which they take away, and use chiefly as amulets for the averting of mischiefs.' Hieronymus the Egyptian, also, who wrote the Phoenician Antiquities, and Mnaseas, and a great many more, make mention of the same. Nay, Nicholaus of Damascus, in his ninety-sixth book, hath a particular relation about them, where he speaks thus: 'There is a great mountain in Armenia, over Minyas, called Baris, upon which it is reported that many who fled at the time of the Deluge were saved; and that one who was carried in an ark came on shore upon the top of it; and that the remains of the timber were a great while preserved. This might be the man about whom Moses, the legislator of the Jews wrote.'"

God had the Flood leave many signs on the face of the earth to remind men how much He hated iniquity. However, modern uniformitarian geologists attempt to explain the signs in terms of currently operative, relatively mild geological processes acting over millions of years. But many of the geological features of the earth give such strong evidences of catastrophic processes having been at work that uniformitarian geologists are forced to admit the occurrence of catastrophes they cannot explain. Yet they resolutely refuse to explain the features as being caused by a worldwide flood because that reeks of religion and science must distance itself from religion. There are several geological phenomena that are certain signs of the Deluge; ossiferous fissures, fossil lakes, coal beds, oil deposits, fossils, and mammoth remains.

Ossiferous fossils are found in many places throughout the world. They are rents in the earth, some measuring 140 to 300 feet deep, filled with the incomplete remains of many different animals mixed together. In Agate Springs, Nebraska such a deposit contains bones of about 9,000 animals such as rhinoceroses, camels, and giant wild boars all jumbled together.

Fossil lakes, for example, in the Tibetan plateau some 16,000 feet high, there are numerous "salt lakes" indicating that this area was once beneath the sea.

Coal beds; the source of all coal is vegetable matter produced by the rapid burial of the lush vegetation of that ancient world during the Flood. Well-preserved plants abound in the rocks that overlie and underlie the coal beds. They are not found in the coal itself because the processes that produced the coal destroyed their forms.

Oil deposits are found in fossiliferous strata, and are a product of organic matter. These deposits were produced during the Flood when huge quantities of living organisms, which manufactured the oil, were rapidly buried. The oil was distilled by the heat and the pressure, and collected in sand between impermeable strata where it remained stored.

Fossils are the remains of living organisms. All kinds of fossils from living and extinct plants and animals have been found throughout the world. In some places a great variety of plant and animal fossils have been found all heaped together like a mountain. Marine fossils are found far inland on mountain tops. The worldwide fossil record is a three-dimensional snapshot of the destruction of the pre-flood world destroyed by water.

Mammoth remains (mammoth were large elephants) were preserved in great numbers encased in the frozen tundra of northern Siberia. They were frozen so quickly that their flesh has been preserved intact. Sub-tropic plants were found undigested in their stomachs. Bears, wolves and prisoners from Siberian concentration camps have fed on their defrosted flesh. Many other kinds of animals were buried with them, including horses, buffaloes, rhinoceroses, oxen and sheep. Their quick burial in loam or gravel occurred during the Flood. Their quick freezing was probably caused by a catastrophic change in climatic conditions brought on by the Flood.

Some object to the idea of a worldwide flood, as described in Genesis, that destroyed both man and beast together because no human fossils are found mixed in with the animal fossils. The answer to this objection is that, in the beginning, animals were far more numerous than humans on the earth (Adam and Eve being the only two). So the numbers of animals exceeded the numbers of men by orders of magnitude. When the Flood waters came men trapped at lower elevations would have been drowned and their bodies devoured by fish, or quickly decayed. Men in higher elevations would have been prey for the multitude of large beasts crowding in from lower elevations, so it is quite reasonable that there were not many human remains left for fossilization. Some human fossils have been found, and also, fossilized dinosaur and giant human footprints have been found together indicating men and dinosaurs were contemporaries, thus undermining the timetable needed for evolution to have occurred.

One supposed inconsistency concerning the Genesis Flood account concerns the number of pairs of each animal taken on to the ark. Genesis 6:19 speaks of two of every sort of animal taken on board the ark, while Genesis 7:2-3 speaks of seven pairs of all clean animals taken aboard. Some critics claim therefore that these two accounts are contradictory, yet they overlook the fact that the reason that seven pairs of clean animals were brought aboard was for the sacrifices offered after the Flood as related in Genesis 8:20.

# DOCTRINE SIXTEEN

## All the races of men on earth today descended from the three sons of Noah.

S cripture and Tradition clearly teach that all people on earth today are descended from the three sons of Noah and that God multiplied the languages of man in response to the rebellion at Babel, after which postdiluvian man dispersed throughout the world.

God made a covenant with Noah, his sons, their descendants and every living creature. He promised never again to send a flood to destroy the earth. The sign of this covenant was the rainbow (Gen. 9:8-17). In Genesis 9:2-3 God told Noah that the beasts of the world would dread man and that they would become food for him. This is also something new. In the antediluvian world there was much greater harmony between man and beast than there is in the post-diluvian world. Antediluvian man did not eat animal flesh because God had not given it to him to eat. Men did not need it then because there was a great variety of plant foods that satisfied all nourishment needs. God made two prohibitions: eating meat with blood in it and murder (Gen.9:4-6). The first was intended as a sign of respect for the lives of animals, which are gifts from God. Leviticus 17:10-16 reaffirms the prohibition not to eat blood because blood represented the life of an animal. Blood is an apt symbol for the soul because it permeates the whole body just as the soul is completely present everywhere in the body, and is as necessary for life as is the soul. So blood can be considered as the material counterpart of the soul. The second prohibition upheld the right to life of all men, because they are created in God's image.

Murder was to be paid for by the life of the person who committed it. This command was also something new. (God did not demand that Cain give up his life in payment for Abel's life.) It became the most fundamental statute in the Law of Nations, that common body of laws recognized by the nations descended from Noah's sons.

Everyone in the world today is descended from three lines—those of Shem, Ham and Japheth, Noah's three sons. The line of Shem was especially blessed because God chose it to be the one to hold on to the true worship of Him. It is the line in which the Redeemer was born. Noah prophesied that God would enlarge the line of Japheth. His descendants would be numerous, and they would "dwell in the tents of Shem", that is, they would share in the spiritual blessings of Shem. Noah cursed Ham because of his immodesty and gross disrespect, declaring that his offspring would be the slaves of the offspring of Shem and Japheth (Gen. 9:18-27). St. Ephrem summarizes the fulfillment of Noah's prophecies: "Japheth increased and became powerful in his inheritance in the north and in the west. And God dwelt in the tent of Abraham, the descendant of Shem, and Canaan became their slave when in the days of Joshua son of Nun, the Israelites destroyed the dwelling places of Canaan and pressed their leaders into bondage."

Genesis 10 contains the original table of nations. It is an authoritative account of how the families of Noah's three sons grew and spread throughout the world. Like the antediluvian genealogy, the men mentioned were not the only sons of their fathers. They are only those who became the patriarchs of nations. St Augustine reckoned seventy-two such nations. He points out that Scripture does not proclaim the devotion to God of anyone between Noah and Abraham and wonders if there was an interruption in the true worship of God during that period, concluding that it is difficult to know the answer. However, it seems that the patriarchs between Shem and Abram did preserve true worship because Genesis 12 says Abram is familiar with and pleasing to God though some of his ancestors worshipped idols. At this point Fr. Warkulwiz gives a listing of the patriarchs and their ages from Noah to Abram; Abram was born just two years after Noah died at the age of 950.

There is a persistent decline in longevity from Noah to Abram which continued beyond Abraham in biblical history until it levels off at "threescore and ten." It seems that some kind of natural process may have been at work that gradually decreased man's lifetime. Perhaps a change in plant nutrients or a loss of genetic information occurred due to the Flood as much of the antediluvian gene pool would have been lost, and possibly, close inbreeding after the Flood may have had a negative effect.

The historian Josephus said that Noah's sons were the first to move down from the mountains and on to the plain of Shinar, but gradually others followed them albeit reluctantly. According to Genesis 11:3, they began to build cities. Originally all spoke the same language. God had commanded them to disperse and fill the earth, but after settling in Shinar they resisted this command saying, "Come, let us build ourselves a city, and a tower with its top in the heavens, and let us make a name for ourselves, lest we be scattered upon the whole face of the earth" (Gen. 11:4). According to Ussher's chronology, the building of the tower of Babel was 105 years after the Flood. According to Josephus, Nimrod was the instigator of this rebellion and St. Augustine concurred. Genesis 10:8-12 says Nimrod ". . . was the first on earth to be a mighty man. He was a mighty hunter before the Lord . . ." and lists Babel and the several other cities that Nimrod built. St. Augustine and St Ephrem interpret the passage to mean that Nimrod was against the Lord, and St John Chrysostom qualified this by saying that in the end Nimrod became corrupted by his own power.

God foiled the scheme of those who built the tower of Babel by multiplying their languages, from which all languages of today are descended. The loss of their common language caused divisions and led to the dispersal of the various peoples of the seventy-two nations. St. Ephrem said this led to war breaking out: ". . . because of their new languages . . . war broke out . . . . It was Nimrod who scattered them. It was also he who seized Babel and became its first ruler." St Jerome said that God dispersed the nations for their own welfare so that they would not have to endure each other. St. Lawrence of Brindisi adds that those who spoke the same language as Nimrod remained with him in Babel and preserved the city.

All the population of the world dispersed from the plain of Shinar. Those that remained close to Shinar developed high civilizations. Settlements on new frontiers were primitive until natural resources were discovered and exploited. The so-called Stone Age, Bronze Age and Iron Age are not true historical periods. Rather, they are the inventions of evolutionists who believe that mankind gradually gained skills with these materials. Archaeological evidence indicates that bronze and iron were fashioned in the earliest Sumerian and Egyptian civilizations. Stone implements were used by those who either lost knowledge of those skills or did not have access to the metals. Also, archaeologists have discovered stone products side by side with products of copper or bronze.

The first nations mentioned in Genesis 10:2-5 are those descended from Japheth. His descendants went north, west and east into Europe and Russia while others headed southeast to Iran and India. Seven sons of Japheth are mentioned as founders of nations. Josephus made a listing of those nations. He also names nations founded by Japheth's grandsons. For example, Tarshish, founder of the Tharsians, whose home area was later known as Cilicia, the major city of which is Tarsus. Then there is Kittim, who settled on Cyprus. The earliest Europeans kept meticulous records of their descent from Japheth. Genesis 10:6-20 lists the nations descended from Ham (Hamites). These went south, east and west from Shinar and eventually developed into the nonwhite nations in both the eastern and western hemispheres. Some of these nations were Cush, Egypt, Put and Canaan, as well as the people known as the Philistines, who occupied Palestine in David's time.

Genesis 10 also lists the lineage of Shem. Josephus further develops it as follows: "Shem, the third son of Noah, had five sons, who inhabited the land that began at Euphrates, and reached to the Indian Ocean. Elam left behind him the Elamites, the ancestors of the Persians. Ashur lived at the city of Nieve and named his subjects Assyrians, who became the most fortunate of nations, beyond others. Arphaxad named the Arphaxadites, who are now called Chaldeans. Aram had the Aramites, which the Greeks call Syrians. Laud founded the Laudites, which are now called the Lydians. Of the four sons of Aram, Uz founded Trachonitis and Damascus; this country lies between Palestine and Celesyria. Ul founded Armenia . . . ." The line of Arphashad leads to Abram and to Jesus Christ. The language of Aram, Aramaic, was adopted by many nations and became the lingua franca of the ancient Near East. It was the native tongue of Christ. The Semites did not migrate much and even today most still live in the Near East.

God's punishments are blessings in disguise. They are not vindictive, but corrective. God punishes out of love and mercy, not anger. When God took away from men a single language, He took away a means of achieving prosperity. Unity of language facilitates commerce, education, travel, and technological innovation, which are all conducive to building up material wealth. But material prosperity becomes a substitute for God. Immersed in prosperity, men tend to praise their own cleverness in achieving it rather than to thank God for providing it. And they look to their own material wealth for their well-being rather than to God. Eventually they fall away from their devotion to God into idolatry, which is accompanied by social disharmony. Unity in language is also conducive to the accumulation of military and political power by tyrants. With a single language all mankind was susceptible to being subjected to dynasty after dynasty of despots. Perhaps God ordered men to disperse throughout the world to prevent them from engaging in continual civil wars on the one hand, or from being enslaved in a one-world tyranny on the other. The first privation would bring on the second. For anarchy produces tyranny. History has shown that people accept a tyrannical centralized government as a lesser evil than anarchy.

When men did not disperse as God commanded, he forced them to do so by multiplying their languages. This was an act of love. God wanted to foster in each of the nations an identity and an independent spirit that would maintain a balance-of-power in the world and counter any tendency to domination by a centralized world power. The various languages He gave the nations would insulate them to some extent so that they might develop their own distinct cultures in which they would exercise their own distinctive talents. Thus God prevented an homogenized humanity and, instead, provided for a wonderful variety of peoples, cultures and traditions that would fulfill the potentials of the human species. Since God does nothing in vain, it is reasonable to suppose that He gave each nation a language with a vocabulary and structure specifically tailored to the needs and aptitudes of its people.

After the Flood, when the world was ready to be re-occupied, God told Noah to lead his family out of the ark into the new world. In Genesis 8:17 God also instructed Noah: "Bring forth with you every living thing that is with you of all flesh—birds and animals and every creeping thing that creeps on the earth—that they may breed abundantly on the earth, and be fruitful and multiply on the earth." The animals spread throughout the whole world. Many crossed land-bridges that then existed to the western hemisphere and Australia. Others migrated across water on floating debris. Some were not able to adapt permanently to the harsh environments of the new world and became extinct after a number of generations. This was the fate of the dinosaurs. Dinosaurs (dragons) were contemporaries of post-diluvian man. The literature of early civilizations testifies to this, and pictographs and petroglyphs of dinosaurs have been found on walls of caves and canyons. These later are documented in modern day books.

Archaeology, bearing on biblical questions, mostly involves the excavations of *tells* (Arabic for hills) in the Middle East. A tell is an artificial mound that conceals the debris of ancient cities, one built on another. In many places a city was destroyed by warfare or natural disaster and a new city rebuilt on the remains, this occurring a number of times during the course of centuries. The site supposed to be that of ancient Troy, for example, had nine levels containing the remains of nine different cities. A layer in which archaeological material (artifacts and the remains of houses) is found is called a stratum. Tells vary from 50-150 feet in elevation and tend to be flat-topped. Artifacts such as pottery, cuneiform tablets, jewelry and monuments found in a tell give archaeologists insights about the cultures of the various people that lived there. These items can be dated back to 1000 BC with reasonable accuracy and back to 2500 BC within a hundred years. But beyond that the dating methods are subject to significant errors.

No credible archaeological dating of an ancient civilization antedates 3000 BC, and therefore all fall within the framework of biblical chronology. Earlier dates have been assigned to various cultures or civilizations; but they are based on radiocarbon or geological methods rather than written human records, which are much more certain. The oldest civilizations according to archaeological reckoning are located in the Near East and were quite advanced with some form of written communication. They used fire, built houses, played music and practiced some form of religion. All of this is in accordance with the biblical record. The oldest archaeological find is believed to be Old Sumer, which is located at the southeastern corner of the Fertile Crescent. Many scholars believe that Nimrod founded it. The facts discovered by archaeologists are in perfect agreement with Sacred Scripture, although their interpretations are not always so. The historical conclusions of archaeologists, when based on archaeological information alone, are often subjective and inconclusive. This has been shown clearly in the theories of archaeologists about the Trojan War. After analyzing various opinions on the subject one commentator observed, "There can never be a final word, only a new interpretation by each generation in terms of its own dreams and needs." So archaeology must look to Sacred Scripture as the basis and guide for the interpretation of its data when it deals with the earliest civilizations. If it doesn't it will quickly lose its way and get lost in false historical conclusions.

One of the objections made to the biblical account of the confusion of languages in Genesis is that scientists "know" that the different languages did not come about in that way. They say language is a highly developed form of animal signaling that probably developed in eastern Africa about 100,000 years ago. Supposedly humans discovered that they were able to produce a range of sounds that could be used to communicate information to other humans. The contrary view is that linguists themselves admit that they have no direct knowledge of the origins and early development of language, nor can they even imagine how such knowledge could be obtained. They can only speculate. The prominent linguist Noam Chomsky denied any relationship between human language and animal signaling saying, ". . . human language appears to be a unique phenomenon, without significant analogue in the animal world." Animal signals are fixed, limited, and instinctively used. Human communications are variable, unlimited and freely used. A second objection raised to the Genesis account regarding language is that archaeological finds have been judged by radiocarbon dating to be as old as 50,000 years. Thus science has invalidated biblical chronology and the history that goes along with it. However, a critical examination of the radiocarbon method and its calibration by tree-ring dating shows that this second objection is false.

The method of radiocarbon dating is used to date something that was once a living organism or was once part of a living organism. While the organism was still living it ingested the radioisotope carbon-14, which is produced in the upper atmosphere by cosmic rays, along with the stable isotope carbon-12. While it was living, it remained in equilibrium with the carbon reservoir in the atmosphere and the ratio of the number of carbon-14 atoms to the number of carbon-12 atoms that it contained remained constant. After the organism died, it ingested no new carbon. As time went on the carbon-14 decayed into nitrogen-14 but the carbon-12 remained intact. So the ratio of the number of carbon-14 to carbon-12 atoms decreased. This ratio is measured and is used to calculate how far in the past the organism died.

In this method it is, first of all, assumed that the ratio of carbon-14 to carbon-12 in the atmospheric carbon reservoir is uniform throughout the earth and constant in time. The latter implies that the rate of production of carbon-14 in the atmosphere has remained constant over time. Atmospheric contamination by fossil fuels must be considered because it could have significantly altered the ratio. To correct for this potential error, the estimated ratio before the industrial revolution is used as a standard. However, there are indications that the concentration of carbon-14 in the atmosphere varied significantly even before the industrial revolution. To account for variations in the atmospheric reservoir, the measure has been calibrated by the technique of tree-ring dating, but the improvement in reliability it gives is quite limited. Also to be taken into account are other effects that could have altered the carbon ratio in a specimen. There are processes such as ground water leaching and bacterial reaction that can alter the carbon ratio, so care is taken to choose samples free of contamination. The method is reliable only for measurements up to a few thousand years. Some scientists and historians do not trust the method for dating items beyond 1000

BC. The dates it gives often differ from dates derived by historical methods.

One subtle assumption of radiocarbon dating is that life has been on earth long enough for the rate-of-decay of carbon-14 in dead organisms to equal the rate-of-production of carbon-14 in the atmosphere. The beginning of production of carbon-14 from nitrogen-14 by the bombardment of neutrons in the atmosphere is like turning on the faucet in a bathtub. Its accumulation in living organisms is like the accumulation of water in the bathtub. Its decay in dead organisms is like there being a leak in the bathtub plug. As the water level rises, the leak rate increases because of the increased pressure. After a while, the water will reach a level at which the rate of water pouring into the tub equals the rate of water draining out. Thus equilibrium is reached, and the water level in the tub remains constant. Measurements have shown that equilibrium has not been reached in the case of carbon-14. Even Willard Libby, who invented the method and wrote a monograph on it, recorded a difference in rates of about 20%, which he dismissed as experimental error. Later estimates gave even higher discrepancies. If those discrepancies are taken seriously they imply that the carbon-14 "faucet" was turned on only several thousand years ago, implying either Creation or some catastrophe took place at that time.

Radiocarbon dating has proved much less precise for dating ancient Near-East civilizations than historical chronology. Therefore it is little used when historical data is available. Despite this, it is still used to establish dates when historical data is not available. Enthusiastic proponents of this method claim that it is useful for dating up to 50,000 years. This, of course, greatly exceeds the range of biblical chronology. In addition, it exceeds the competence of the method, even if the earth were that old. There are no 50,000 year-old historical records or trees that can be used to calibrate it for such extreme measurements. It would not even be capable of dating antediluvian finds, if any archaeological find could be certainly established as such, because the Flood would probably have greatly affected the production and distribution of carbon-14. The fact that there is practically no carbon-14 in coal suggests that there was no carbon-14 in the atmosphere before the Flood. Furthermore, for measurements of 50,000 years age, the carbon-14 concentration would be very low (0.2% of maximum) because 50,000 years is close to nine half-lives of carbon-14. Such measurements require very sensitive instruments and very pure samples.

Interestingly, Willard Libby admitted that the radiocarbon dating-method lent support to the biblical revelation that human civilization appeared abruptly on earth only several thousand years ago: "The first shock that Dr. Arnold and I had was that our advisers informed us that history extended back only 5,000 years. We had thought initially that we would be able to get samples all along the curve back to 30,000 years, put the points in, and then our work would be finished. You read books and find statements that 'such and such a society or archaeological site is 20,000 years old.' We learned rather abruptly that these numbers, these ancient ages, are not known; in fact, it is about the time of the first dynasty in Egypt that the last historical date of any real certainty has been established."

The science of dendrochronology, or tree-ring dating, is also used in archaeology, both in its own right and to provide calibration for radiometric dating. It is based on the fact that each year a tree adds a ring to its growth, the size and composition of which depends on that year's weather and environmental conditions. Trees growing in the same area will have matching sequences, so scientists have been able gradually to construct an absolute chronology by overlapping sequences of successively older ring patterns. The ring patterns are those in pieces of wood taken from living trees and old timbers found at various places. From these overlapping sequences a master chart can be drawn up. The composers of the master chart must take great care in matching the pieces together. They must be skilled at recognizing the distinguishing features of ring patterns so that correct matches are made. A sample from an ancient wooden beam from an archaeological site can be sent to a laboratory to be compared against the chart to establish its age. By studying the rings of many samples of timber from different sites and strata within a particular region, archaeologists build up an historical sequence. This particular technique is well developed in the American Southwest. In that range the ages it deduces can be compared with historical information.

The oldest known living thing is the Bristlecone Pine. Microscopic study of the growth rings of some living specimens of bristlecone pines in California and Nevada yielded ages from 4600 to 4900 years. That means that they would have sprouted shortly after the great Flood. However, dendrochronologists try to extend the range of the method by looking for matching tree-ring patterns in timbers they think to be even older. In this way sequences derived from the Bristlecone Pine have been extended to 6700 B.C., which corresponds to nearly twice the age of the oldest living specimens. Such extrapolation is difficult, subjective and uncertain.

As mentioned earlier the tree-ring method is used to calibrate radiocarbon dating. The carbon-14/carbon-12 ratios are measured for individual tree rings. From this data a calibration curve is drawn, which supposedly enables the user to compensate for variations in carbon ratio in the atmospheric carbon-reservoir over time. This at best could increase the reliability of the method only to the age of the oldest living trees. It has been pointed out that: "Attempts to derive historical age from radiocarbon age yield increasingly uncertain conjectures for samples older than 2000 years. Tree-ring chronology has been extended from 59 B.C. to approximately 2400 B.C. using the Bristlecone Pine. The growth characteristics of this tree make it unsatisfactory for the establishment of a precise, long-term, growth-ring sequence. Attempts to correlate Bristlecone Pine growth-rings with radiocarbon ages indicate that either ring counting has over-estimated the age of the oldest Bristlecone Pines by 500 to 1000 years, or the relative amount of Carbon-14 in the atmosphere around 2000 B.C. was in the order of 10 percent greater than in A.D. 1850 (the standard year)."

# MEDIEVAL CATHOLIC PERSPECTIVE ON CREATION

## St. Thomas Aquinas and St. Bonaventure on Creation

The technological powers of observation of medieval Catholic scholars were more limited than ours, but they stuck to the observed facts more closely than we do. They were much less speculative about the nature of the cosmos than are modern scientists. And, of course, they deeply respected revealed truth about the world, which modern scientists consider irrelevant. For these reasons their vision of the cosmos was less distorted and more realistic than ours, despite its limitations. They knew that man discovers only what God allows him to discover, that nature reveals only what God permits her to reveal. In contrast, the science idolaters of our age are presumptuous and sophomoric. They think that they know more about the world than they really do and fail to recognize the blind spots in their powers of observation and reasoning, the kinds of blind spots that magicians and charlatans exploit. There are many things that elude the narrow means of investigation that they praise so highly.

One must not fail to realize that the world is holistic, while the human mind, in this world being limited to the reasoning process, functions analytically. Consequently we will never completely comprehend the universe. We will never come to know the world perfectly, though we will always discover more and better ways of using the things in it. With every genuine advance in scientific knowledge, creation becomes more awe-filled, wondrous and mysterious; and it becomes more apparent how little we really know about it. The theology of Creation elaborated by the Fathers of the Church was systematized by the Catholic theologians of the thirteenth century. The traditional Catholic perspective on creation that was formulated by them was adorned with Greek cosmology. It could adopt any cosmology that was consistent with the Genesis account. Following are summaries of the medieval Catholic vision of creation, as was projected by St. Thomas Aquinas (1225-1274) and St. Bonaventure (1225-1274). We will begin with St. Thomas.

St. Thomas believed that the natural world has a religious value. In Chapter 2 of the second book of the "Summa Contra Gentiles" he argued that the consideration of creatures is useful for building up faith in God. He gives four reasons to support his claim. First, "through meditating on His works we are able somewhat to admire and consider the divine wisdom." Second, "this consideration leads us to admire the sublime power of God, and consequently begets in men's hearts a reverence for God." Third, "this consideration inflames the souls of men to the love of the divine goodness." Fourth, "this consideration bestows on man a certain likeness to the divine perfection," because, "to know creatures by the light of divine revelation . . . results in man a certain likeness to the divine wisdom."

In Chapter 3 of the same work he argues that consideration of creatures is also necessary for refuting errors about God because "errors about creatures sometimes lead one astray from the truth of the faith, in so far as they disagree with the true knowledge of God." He says that this happens in several ways. First, "because through ignorance of the nature of creatures men are sometimes so far misled as to deem that which can but derive its being from something else to be the first cause and God, for they think nothing exists besides visible creatures." Second, "because they ascribe to certain creatures that which belongs to God alone . . . . Into this error fell those who ascribe the creation of things, or the knowledge of the future, or the working of miracles to causes other than God." This is the error of today's evolutionists, who attribute powers to creatures that properly belong to God. Third, "because something is withdrawn from the divine power in its working on creatures, through ignorance of the creature's nature." This is evidenced in those who say that there is more than one principle of creation, in those who say that things proceed from God not by the divine will but by necessity, and in those who deny that God can work outside the ordinary course of things. Fourth, "Man, who is led by faith to God as his last end, through ignoring the natures of things, and consequently the order of his place in the universe, thinks himself to be beneath certain creatures above whom he is placed." This the error of those who subject man's will to the stars.

In Chapter 4 St. Thomas considers that philosophers and theologians treat of creatures in different ways. The philosopher is interested in the creatures in themselves, that is, in their natures, whereas the theologian is interested in the relation of creatures to God, especially in how they manifest His glory. Philosophy is the handmaid to theology. For in considering creatures in themselves it leads us from them to the knowledge of God. In St. Thomas' "Writings on the 'Sentences'" he argues, in opposition to Manichean dualism, that there is only one principle of creation, namely, God. He defines creation as production from nothing, from non-being to being. He then goes on to distinguish creation from the eternal generation of God the Son from God the Father: "What a thing has from itself and not from something else is naturally prior in it to that which it has from something else. (In this way creation differs from eternal generation, for it cannot be said that the Son of God, if left to Himself, would not have being, since He receives it from the Father that very same being which the Father has, which is absolute being, not dependent upon anything.)" St. Thomas says that creation as understood by the above two points (creation from nothing and creation from another) can be demonstrated by philosophers.

Subsequently he considers whether agents other than God can create. He says: "being and non-being are separated by an absolute infinity." Therefore the act of creation requires an infinite power, which belongs to God alone. This power cannot be given to any creature because the creature would then be the primary cause of being, which it is not. St. Thomas also considers whether agents other than God are able to cause anything. In other words, he treats the question of whether or not secondary causes had a role in the production of the things of the world. He holds that God alone is the immediate cause of those things that come into being by creation. This includes angels and human souls because these are pure forms, that is, they are not composites, and, as such, cannot be produced by other creatures. God is also the immediate cause of prime matter. Of those things composed of matter and form, God directly created the elements because other material substances are not capable of producing them. Aquinas also held that heavenly bodies, such as the sun, were also directly created because, following Aristotle, he believed that they were composed of an incorruptible substance incapable of being produced by other creatures. Concerning living creatures, Aquinas said that there are some that (by nature) necessarily produce what is similar in species, through the process of generation. Of such creatures "the first members were immediately created by God, such as the first man, the first lion, and so forth. Man, for instance, can only be generated from man."

Aquinas next considers whether the world is eternal. He produces a number of arguments saying that it is and a number of arguments saying that it isn't. He says that there are three positions on the question: First, that God and all other things are eternal; second, that the world and everything other than God began to exist after they had not existed, and that God could not have made an eternal world, not because of a lack of His power, because the world could not have been made eternally since it was created; third, that everything other than God began to exist, but nevertheless the fact that the world has begun to exist cannot be demonstrated but is rather held and believed to be so by divine revelation. He holds the third position, saying: "The reason this question cannot be demonstrated is that the nature of a thing is quite different in its complete being from what it was when it was in the process of being made by its cause. For example, the nature of a man who is already born is different from that of a man while he is still in his mother's womb."

St. Thomas says that what we call "space" is defined by the objects in it and was created with the world; "it ought to be said that before the creation of the world there was no void, as there is none after, because the void is not a simple negation but a privation. Hence, in order that there be a void, as those who suppose that there is one would say, there must be a place or real dimensions, neither of which did exist before the world." As to real and imaginary time he says, ". . . it ought to be said that God precedes the world not only in nature, but also in duration, not, however, in a duration of time, but in a duration of eternity. Before the world there was no time in reality, but in imagination only, because we now imagine that God could have added many years earlier to this finite time, and to all of these earlier years God's eternity would have been present."

Finally Aquinas examines Genesis 1:1, "In the beginning God created the heavens and the earth." In discussing the Trinitarian nature of the Creator he says, "It ought to be said that the designation of being the efficient cause is appropriate to the Father, whereas the designation of being the exemplar cause for a work of art is appropriated to the Son, who is the Wisdom and the Art of the Father." And the goodness of creation is appropriated to the Holy Spirit. By explaining the Creator Trinity he refuted the errors of the Manichees who held there to be more than one creative principle. He defends the interpretation of "in the beginning" as "in the beginning of time" to refute the error of the eternity of the world. And, finally he defends the interpretation of "in the beginning" as "before all things" to defend against the error of those who hold that the visible things were created by God through the mediation of angels. He says that God created everything "in the beginning." He says, ". . . it ought to be said that by 'heavens' is also understood the angelic nature, which is said to dwell in the heavens, and by 'earth' is understood all generable and corruptible things."

Now we consider what St. Bonaventure wrote on these matters. St. Bonaventure, the Seraphic Doctor and his mentor, Alexander of Hales, were the great Franciscan masters of the thirteenth century. Bonaventure's doctrine on creation is found chiefly in his "Commentary on the Sentences" and his "Breviloquium". In his philosophy/theology of creation he generally agreed with Aquinas. Like Aquinas, he generally interpreted Genesis literally unless he felt compelled to do otherwise. "We should especially hold these truths about corporeal nature as regards its becoming: that it was brought into existence in six days so that in the beginning, before any day, God created the heaven and the earth."

He may seem to be contradicting himself by saying on one hand that corporeal nature was brought into existence in "six days" and on the other hand that God created the heaven and earth "before any day." But he goes on to explain. He seems to say that creation per se, that is, the production ex nihilo, took place at the first instant of time. Once heaven and earth came into existence, so did time: "And because creation is from nothing, it was in the beginning before all days as the foundation of all things and of all times."

The works of the first six days were works of "distinction" and "embellishment." During the first three days God made distinct four natures, namely, light, water, air and earth. During the next three days God embellished the earth with things according to the above four natures: the heavenly bodies correspond to light, the fish to water, the birds to air, and the beasts and man to earth. Furthermore, "Though God was able to do all these things instantaneously, He preferred to accomplish them in a series of periods as a distinct and clear representation of power, wisdom and goodness (power corresponding to creation, wisdom to distinction, and goodness to embellishment) . . . ." He does, however, allow room for Augustine's belief that creation, distinction and embellishment all took place at once and that the six days represent stages of angelic consideration; but he clearly prefers the interpretation that he himself has given.

Bonaventure agrees with Aquinas that God did not stop working on the seventh day, but He desisted from the creation of new forms: "On the seventh day, God desisted not from toil or work, for He still worked, but from the creation of new forms because He had done all things either in likeness, as in the case with those things which are propagated, or in a seminal reason, as in the case with those things which are brought into existence in other ways." And like Aquinas he believed that there would have been no Incarnation if there had been no Fall. There are three major exceptions to Bonaventure's general agreement with Aquinas. First, he held that prime matter is not merely that which is undetermined. Rather, he believed that it contained seminal principles, or potentialities, that were infused by God in the beginning. When God creates, He does not produce new essences. Rather, He actualizes that which is potential. Second, he differs from

Thomas on the possibility of an eternal world. St. Thomas held that it cannot be proven by reason alone that the world was not created from eternity. Conversely, St. Bonaventure held that such can be proven by reason alone. The third point of difference concerns the perpetuation of being. They both agree that creatures will cease to exist if God ceases to cause their existence. For Aquinas, only a single act of God is required to bring a creature into existence and maintain it in existence. However, Bonaventure says God performs two different acts. First He gives existence. Then, since the creature is unable to keep itself in existence, God conserves the creature in existence.

In the "Breviloquium" Bonaventure professes Greek cosmology, which was accepted in one form or another by all of Christendom. He says that heavenly bodies influence "the effective production of things generable and corruptible, namely mineral vegetative, and sensitive life and human bodies." But "they are not certain signs of future contingencies, nor do they exert influence upon the freedom of choice through the power of the constellation, which some philosophers say is fate." So he, like other medieval theologians, believed that the stars influenced things on earth. But he, like the others cannot be accused of believing in astrology, as we understand that term today. The influences he spoke of were pure physical causes, not occult influences.

In conclusion, medieval thinking on creation was hardly perfected before it was overwhelmed by Enlightenment ideology and finally came to be ignored by intellectual leaders in the Church, many of whom were either intimidated or awed by the successes of the new sciences. Thus did much of Christendom gradually lose the faith in the literal truth of Genesis 1-11 that was so strongly held by the Fathers and Doctors of the Church and even becoming embarrassed by their teachings. But although the new sciences were able to overshadow traditional Catholic theology on creation, they were unable to undermine it because it sits on a rock-solid foundation, namely, God's word in Sacred Scripture. Nothing that modern science has discovered or can discover is able to shake that foundation. Scientists and scholars must place their faith in Sacred Scripture and accept its guidance if they are to lead their disciplines in the direction of truth.

Catholic scientists and scholars must purge their minds of the idea that the Church will lose her credibility if she rejects uniformitarian geology, evolutionary biology, evolutionary anthropology, and big bang cosmology. The notions which practitioners of these pseudo-sciences advance have not contributed a mite to our understanding of the nature of things or to our technological progress. The great advances in science and technology that we enjoy were brought about by careful observations of nature, here and now, and by technical innovations—not by theories about the past.

Holy Mother Church will increase her credibility many times over if her teachers and preachers once more clearly and confidently profess her traditional theology of creation. And that will help restore moral soundness to Western civilization, because much of the immorality present today can be traced to a false conception of the nature of man, which is rooted in false conceptions about origins. We must go "back to the future" to recover that religious, social, and scientific sanity that was enjoyed by medieval Christendom during the Age of Faith.

1 This *Compendium* was lovingly composed by Brother Charles Madden, O.F.M., Conv., with the approval of Fr. Victor Warkulwiz, the author of the work upon which it is based, *The Doctrines of Genesis 1-11: A Compendium and Defense of Traditional Catholic Theology on Origins* (Caryville, TN: John Paul II Institute of Christian Spirituality, 2010).